THE SECRETS TO GETTING A JOB

the secrets to

GETTING a JOB

Philip Garside

HYLAND HOUSE

First published in Australia in 1997 by
Hyland House Publishing Pty Limited
Hyland House
387-389 Clarendon Street
South Melbourne
Victoria 3205

Reprinted 1997 (twice)

© Philip Garside 1997

National Library of Australia
Cataloguing-in-publication data:

Garside, Philip, 1955– .
The secrets to getting a job.

  ISBN 1 86447 013 5.

  1. Job hunting. 2. Employment interviewing. 3. Resumes
  (Employment). I. Title.

650.14

Typeset in Caslon 11/12pt by Hyland House
Printed in Australia by Australian Print Group

CONTENTS

ACKNOWLEDGEMENTS

Thanks to The Saint, Michael McClure, for your ongoing support. Thanks also to my supporters in the early days: Karen O'Callaghan, Carol McCabe and Bob Hotston.

Thank you to my partner Margaret, whose support, assistance and patience have been legendary.

'Interviews are not about the best person for the job; interviews are about, and can only ever be about, who *appears* to be the best person for the job. From an interview we can only tell who *interviews* best.'

INTRODUCTION

It's my belief that all advice should be treated scep-
tically, and that is how I expect you to treat mine.

This is especially true when talking about job
interviews, because there is no shortage of advice
available—every friend and colleague who knows
you are on the interview treadmill has some advice,
and so does every distant aunt and uncle.

In no time the different bits of advice start to contradict each other and, if you are not careful, you can
end up like a ball in a pinball machine, bouncing
between them all.

I certainly don't want to add to your problems. What I want to do is show you the underlying logic of *my* advice. Perhaps explaining how this book came to be written will help you decide how much to trust it.

It was during the recession of the early 1980s that I became interested in employment interview techniques. Although not as bad as the 1990s recession, it was still hard to find work, and for those with a job, it was hard to be promoted to a higher level.

At the time I was working as a placement officer with an employment service. As you would suppose, a placement officer's main task is to find jobs for people. This involves advising unemployed people and linking them with employers, and during a recession such work can be difficult and tiring.

Although some people don't think so, the vast majority of unemployed people are very keen to find jobs, at least at the beginning of their search—before resentment and despondency set in. It is upsetting to be involved with job-seekers as financial pressures build and their ambitions and self-esteem slip away, especially when some become so depressed that they give up altogether and stop trying. Watching this slide from hope to despair has been one of the saddest aspects of my working life.

And it's not only the unemployed who become hopeless; those who are continually overlooked for promotion also give up, and resign themselves to remaining at their current level. This is true even if they believe they are able to take on more responsible work or are more capable than people who are promoted ahead of them. There are few things in life more upsetting than seeing someone with less ability than you get the job you would like to have.

Of course not everything was gloomy during the eighties recession. Some people did get jobs and some did get promoted. Some even moved from one job to another, and they weren't necessarily people with special skills. If you asked them why they left their last job, they might reply, 'Didn't like the boss'; 'I felt my work wasn't receiving the recognition it deserved'; or even the marvellous, 'I felt like a change'.

These responses sound quite frivolous at a time of high unemployment: you might think that these were people who either didn't really want to work, or who had such valued skills that they could afford to be choosy. And it is true that some who gave such replies couldn't find a new job. However, many did manage to find new work, sometimes almost immediately, and not all of them had great skills.

So in the middle of a depression some people were desperate for employment and couldn't find any, while others moved freely from job to job. Why? What was the difference between the two groups?

It wasn't ability or the desire to work. Some with tremendous ability and skills were unemployed for long periods while frantic for work. **The main difference was the ability to interview well.** Those who could were able to get jobs or be promoted. Those who couldn't, remained unemployed or overlooked.

This is because the interview is not, and never has been, about the best person for the job, or about ability, skills, or the desire to work. It can't be: there is no way of knowing from an interview who is the best person for the job. Interviews are about, and can only be about, who *appears* to be the best person for the job. From an interview we can only tell who interviews best.

The only way to be sure the best person gets the job would be to give each applicant a trial in the job and see who performs best, an unlikely and impractical solution. If the best person does get the job through the interview process it is merely coincidence or good luck.

Of course many interviewers would disagree with me and argue passionately that they are able to choose the best person, but there is a world of difference between the best person and the person who *appears* to be the best. If only I could get this message to everyone who is in despair because they've missed out on jobs, especially those who are thinking of giving up! They have not been tested for their ability to do the job they're aiming at; they have failed only in their ability to interview well. What these people need to do is work at their interview skills.

We all subconsciously recognise that an interview is in fact a game that is being played, or a role that is being acted. We ask, 'How did you perform at the interview?', suggesting that for an interview you learn your lines and you play your part. The trouble is, not everyone has discovered that interviews are a performance, and of those who have, few know which lines to learn.

If interviews are a game, what are the rules? If they are a performance, what are the lines of the script? I decided to research the answers to these questions. After successfully applying for funding, I arranged to sit in on as many interviews as possible. They covered a wide range of employers and of jobs, over a hundred in all: private sector, public sector, junior and senior, skilled, unskilled and professional job interviews.

I took detailed notes about what had impressed the interviewer and what had not. I soon realised that there was a pattern to being successful at an interview. The rules became quite clear.

As I used this pattern to coach people during the succeeding years I found that the rules remained constant regardless of the position applied for. The content might vary but the structure remained the same for all kinds of jobs—whether manual, technical, professional or management positions. I also found that there was only a loose connection between what interviewers said they wanted from an applicant and the person they chose for the job.

A journalist came to see me after he had failed an interview for a job on a major daily newspaper. He told me about the question which had caused him the biggest problem, and how he had answered it. Then I told him how I would have answered the question. He smiled and said, 'I didn't know you had a background in journalism.' 'I don't,' I said, 'other than a vague general knowledge. What I do have is a background in answering questions.'

Here is another example, which shows that interview skills can be learned, and that the interview process can be manipulated to your advantage. I once coached a bricklayer for a position as a trainee council building inspector. He was doing an evening course to gain the necessary qualification, but he wasn't good at expressing himself, and so he didn't think he could ever interview well. And it was particularly important for him to interview well, because he was trying to make a career change from outdoor trades work to an indoors technical and administrative position, a transition that is difficult to achieve.

We worked together for about eight hours, which is a long time to coach someone for an interview. It was a hard grind, but suddenly the penny dropped: he seemed to understand what I had been trying to teach him about an interview's structures and rules. He grinned, and said confidently, 'Ask me a question; any question!' I asked one of the questions we had been practising. He answered well, then said, 'Ask me something we haven't practised.' I tried some new questions and he handled them well also.

I was very pleased, but he went further, insisting, 'Ask me a question about any job!!' I tried him out, saying 'You are going for an accountant's position and you get asked the following question...', and then, 'You are going for a job as a child-care attendant and...'. In each case he gave a good answer. Of course he had no detailed knowledge of the particular jobs, so a lot of the technical detail was invented and wrong, but basically his answers were sound.

The next week he was successful in his interview, and was chosen from a field of six applicants. Part of his success was due to my teaching, not only of rules, but because I had guessed seven of the nine questions the interviewer would ask, and had helped him put together good answers. Another part of his success was due to the confidence our work together had given him.

At our debriefing session after the interview he said two things.

First, that he couldn't believe how easy it was: when the interviewers kept asking questions he had prepared for, he could hardly keep from bursting out laughing. Second, he was angry because he knew that if I had gone for the job I would have beaten him, and I knew nothing about being a building inspector! True, but I do know a lot about answering questions.

Unfortunately, the bricklayer lost his new job after a few months because he could not get used to working in an office, and his literacy skills weren't good enough to write reports to the standard required. His report-writing skill was not tested at the interview. So the would-be building inspector returned to bricklaying, at least happy that he had given his ambition his best shot. The last I heard, he was being sought out by friends and family to help them with their job interviews.

This story also shows why I am cynical about the interview process. I have coached many people into jobs they have lost a short time later. I can help them past the interview, but I can't give them the skills to do the job.

If this were a book on how to play tennis you would not expect to become a better tennis player just from reading it. You would expect to learn how to practise to develop your skills and improve your game. In the same way, you should not expect to be better at interviews the minute you finish this book, but you will learn how to improve with practice. Remember that if you are unhappy with the way you interview, but after reading the book you do not try to make changes, then you can't hope to improve.

Finally, I should confess that I do not like the interview system. It seems to me to be irrational. There is a vacant position, and to decide who will fill it a competition is held. The applicant who interviews best wins the position, even though the skills demonstrated at the interview will never be used again in the day-to-day work of that job.

Many times supposedly vacant positions are advertised, there is a selection process, and the person chosen is an internal applicant, or the cousin of the plant manager, who was always going to get the job. It would be a lot cheaper and less hurtful if the organisation didn't raise the hopes of other applicants, and just made the appointment without going through the charade of a supposedly open process.

In this book I assume that the process is open, and I focus on the person the interviewers will choose, not what they say they want. For this reason some of my advice may contradict what other people have told you. But if being interviewed is an art, as I believe it to be, and not a science, right and wrong is a matter of opinion. I will try to back up my opinions with examples and reasons, so that you can make your own decision about whether I am right or wrong.

One of the reasons that I think I am right is the number of people who, with my assistance, have got the job they were seeking. Not only that, but they gained in self-confidence, and regained some control over their lives. I have seen the damage the interview system does to good workers who can't get work or improve their position because they interview poorly. They simply don't know the lines in the script or the rules of the game. This book makes the lines and rules available to everyone. I hope that with practice everyone who reads it will be able to say, 'Ask me a question, any question, … any job!'

Chapter 1

HOW THE INTERVIEWER SEES IT

There are many kinds of interviews.

Some are formal, conducted by one or more people to a set format, with a list of questions which are asked of each applicant.

At the other end of the scale there are informal interviews, usually conducted by one person, which often take the form of a chat over a cup of coffee.

In between, there can be great variety. There are interviews with no questions, where the interviewer simply says, 'You have forty minutes to convince me that you should get the job.' Other interviewers will do most of the talking. Some interviewers know exactly what they are looking for, others are unsure and half-hope the interviewee will tell them. There are skilled interviewers who know how to conduct a fair interview and give each applicant an equal opportunity to show their qualifications; there are others who have no idea at all how to conduct an interview. There are even times when you have not applied for a job, but your boss says, 'Did you know that Smith over at Plant B is resigning?', giving you a chance to suggest that you would be good for that job.

So never assume that all interviews are the same—far from it. What is always the same are the needs of each interviewee. Each must make their claim for the position they hope to win in the most convincing way possible, regardless of the form the interview takes. Sometimes this means that the interviewee must take some control of the process, either overtly or covertly.

In this book I have used the 'set question and answer' interview to pass on my advice, as it is easier and clearer for both myself and the reader. If your interview is not in this question and answer format, the book's ideas, techniques and information are still valid, but will need to be adapted to the particular style of interview.

Let's start by considering how the interviewer looks at things. How would you decide between applicants if you were the interviewer? It's worth keeping in mind that most interviewers are not able to make a distinction between the best person for the job and the person who *appears* to be the best for the job.

If you have a job vacancy, you first place an advertisement in the Positions Vacant section of a newspaper and wait for responses. If you had put your telephone number in the ad the calls would probably have tied up your switchboard for hours, so you state in the ad that you will only accept written applications. Even so, there may be dozens or even hundreds of applications.

To cut down on the number who apply you may use a qualifier such as 'five years' experience necessary'. **Never be deterred from applying for a job because you don't have the specified amount of experience**; it is better to apply and see if the employer rules you out.

Suppose that forty people apply in writing. To reduce the number interviewed still further, the employer makes a short list. That is, you make a series of judgements based on matching the applications with your needs to decide who to interview. Let's say that you decide to interview ten people from among those who sent in written applications.

At the end of the day, one applicant will have a job, and nine will not. To put it another way, there will be one winner and nine losers, or thirty-nine losers if you count the original applicants who weren't asked to come for an interview.

How have you made your decision? Write down a list of the factors which will help you to choose one person over the other nine. This is a task which I often give the groups I am coaching. The sorts of lists they come up with usually look something like this:

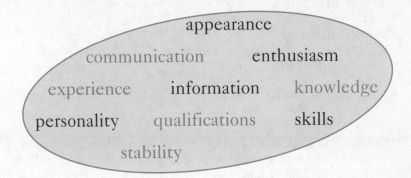

appearance

communication   enthusiasm

experience   information   knowledge

personality   qualifications   skills

stability

If I asked for negative factors, which might be called discrimination, they could be:

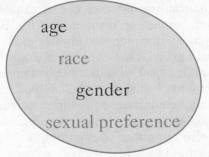

age

race

gender

sexual preference

It is against the law to discriminate in these ways, but it would be naïve not to recognise that some people think in such terms. **If you ever believe that you have missed out on a job for discriminatory reasons that are against the law, complain loud and long to whoever will take up your case**—that is the only way such practices can be stopped.

The list given above is fairly accurate in terms of what most interviewers would say they were looking for in a new employee, although they would probably add two more items: 'achievement' and 'leadership', with the last usually restricted to supervisory positions or jobs that may lead to becoming a supervisor. If we add these, the top list can be split into two types of factors.

List One: *List Two:*

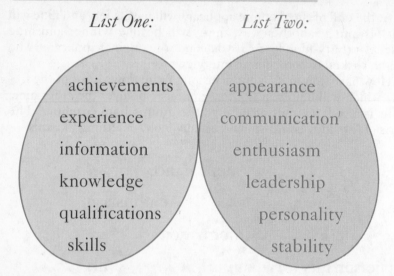

achievements   appearance

experience   communication

information   enthusiasm

knowledge   leadership

qualifications   personality

skills   stability

Although these lists don't include every factor that every interviewer might take into account, they do represent the factors which
most employers list when asked what they are looking for.
Personality is often described as 'someone who will "fit in"'.'Fit in?'
I ask, 'What do you mean by that?' The reply is usually, 'Oh, you
know, someone who will "fit in"!' In other words, it is a 'feeling'
about somebody, not something which people can define.

I call List One the 'merit' or 'competency' list. Be careful about
the word 'competency'. It sometimes implies mediocrity. If you go
to a restaurant and I ask you what the service was like, you might
reply 'competent', if it wasn't good, but not bad enough to complain
about. This is not what I mean by the 'competency' list. What I
mean is that you can demonstrate at an interview that you have the
listed factors—skills, knowledge, experience, etc.

If interviews were just about competency, I wouldn't object to
them so much. Competency involves objective attributes which
are testable. It is possible to test an applicant's skills, discover
their experience, ask questions to determine their knowledge and
information. It is a simple matter to check qualifications, and by
talking to referees to verify an applicant's achievements.

But surprisingly, none of these factors in list one are of much
importance to the person being interviewed, because no matter how
well you compare on all of them, **they are not the factors which
will make the interviewer choose you.** This is not only surprising, but disappointing to many interviewees, who have used their
energies at their interview displaying the factors in the first list.

There are two reasons why these merit factors have little value
for you at an interview. First, forty applicants were short-listed

down to ten. Most short-listing processes sort through the applicants for the skills, experience and achievements on list number one. Although short-listing isn't always completely fair, it is the fairest part of the interviewing process, and the good news is that if you are granted an interview, you know that someone has decided that you have enough of the competency factors to do the job. You are a contender. The bad news is, so are the other nine applicants. Someone has also decided that they too have enough of the competency factors to do the job. Therefore the ten of you look quite similar in these areas, and it is hard for the interviewers to distinguish between you.

The second reason why competency factors are less important than they might seem is illustrated by the number of times I, and probably all of us, have at some stage worked with someone who has had ten years' experience—and who was hopeless. There might be staff with eighteen months' experience who were more competent. **Experience alone is a poor measure of competency**.

Experience is only time spent seat-warming, and in itself has no value. It is a sad fact that for some people ten years' experience is one year's experience multiplied by ten. They know nothing more at the end of ten years than they did at the end of their first year. In fact, I have worked with some people for whom ten years' experience is six months' experience, twenty times over.

If you look through the Saturday newspapers there will be hundreds, if not thousands, of jobs asking for experience: two years' experience, five years' experience, a minimum of ten years' experience. But I've been in a personnel department when such advertisements are being prepared. Someone stands up and says,

> *'I'm writing that ad for the vacant position. How much experience are we looking for? I was thinking two years.'*
> *'No; make it five.'*
> *'OK.'*

These arbitrary experience qualifications have nothing to do with merit; they may actually prevent the organisation from getting the best person for the job. All they do is make it easier for the staff in the personnel section. The following Saturday, a person who would be an excellent applicant reads the advertisement and thinks, 'Damn it, they are looking for five years' experience and I've only got two', without realising just how close they were to being eligible.

I have seen many thousands of jobs asking for experience. But I have not seen one single employer choose experience above all else, nor have I ever coached anyone who went for a job where the employer chose experience. Not once! What they do choose are the lessons you have learned. **The only value of experience is in the lessons learned from it.** Before going for an interview you need to translate your experience into the lessons you have learned from your years of work.

For those of us applying for positions outside our direct experience, or trying to change career direction completely, this translation of experience into lessons learned can be very helpful. I don't advocate telling lies at interviews, but I do believe in presenting the truth in the best possible light. That is your task at the interview: to present yourself in the best possible way.

I coached a woman who had a very simple goal in life. She wanted to work in the retail area, as a shop assistant. She had a lot of experience of this, as she had been a shopper for many years. Unfortunately most retail outlets don't recognise experience on the other side of the counter, much to their own detriment.

When I heard that she had no experience we had the following conversation:

> *'You've had no experience whatsoever?'*
> *'No, none at all.'*
> *'Not even helping out in the canteen at your children's school?'*
> *'No, not even that. The closest I've come is that for a half-day each year for the last three years, I've helped at the church fête by working on the jumble sale stall.'*

I smiled. Later when I wrote her résumé, I said that she had had retail experience over a three-year period. Technically, this is not a lie. She gained an interview, and when the question of her experience was raised at the interview, she immediately focused on the lessons learned. She got the lessons right, and got the job, which was with a large up-market retail chain. In the end they really didn't want experience—they said they did, but really they wanted the lessons learned.

The same is true of educational qualifications. A degree, a certificate or a diploma may help you to gain an interview, but they are of little further use unless you can show the potential employer how they are a benefit.

Too often interviewees recite their skills, knowledge or qualifications as though reading from their résumé without showing how they would make these factors valuable in the position they are applying for. In other words, **having skills is of little use at an interview; having knowledge is of little use at an interview; having experience is of little use at an interview: being able to demonstrate that you can use your skills, knowledge or experience for the benefit of the employer is everything.**

The only exception is achievements, which can be of great

value if presented correctly. In an interview the true value of any achievement is as a vehicle to demonstrate how you can, and have, used your abilities to benefit an employer.

There is one quality which rarely appears in the list which the groups I coach suggest, and which employers never mention to me, and yet it is a major influence in their decision making. That is represented by the old-fashioned word 'wisdom'. The definition for 'wisdom' in my *Concise Oxford Dictionary* is: 'Being wise; (possession of) experience and knowledge together with the power of applying them critically or practically ...' It is not enough to merely possess the competency factors; one must be able to use them. Other such factors of real value are 'insight' and 'understanding'.

One of the sad experiences of working in my field is being reminded of a very disappointing fact: the nicer an applicant is, the worse that applicant will perform at an interview. Although this is not always the case, thank goodness, it happens far too often to ignore. The problem is that when nice people hear a question at an interview, their first thought is, 'What is the "right answer"?' Then they earnestly and honestly present the 'right answer' to the best of their ability. This approach is naïve. I can assure you that **there are no right answers at an interview.** There are only right approaches. Interviews are not oral exams.

I have seen people come out of an interview very optimistic about their chances: 'They asked me nine questions, and I got eight right, so I must have a chance!', while in fact, they interviewed dreadfully, and have absolutely no chance of getting the job.

The people who do well at interviews have a different approach. When they are asked a question at an interview their first thought is not 'What's the right answer?', but 'How do I best use this question to my advantage?' Trying to get the 'right' answer usually means offering knowledge and information. Good interviewees use the question to demonstrate wisdom, insight and understanding, because these are what interviewers really want to discover.

As you will see when we go through the questions and answers later, each question offers the chance to present either knowledge and information or wisdom, insight and understanding. Every time, wisdom, insight and understanding will be successful. This is why I say that information can actually damage your performance at an interview. Or to be more accurate, relying solely on information can be damaging. But even when wisdom is added to List One, you've only fought half the battle. The other half of the battle is List Two.

If List One is the testable list, List Two is the detestable list. It covers areas which are subjective, the realm of opinion, emotion and feeling. Many times when I've asked an interviewer why they chose someone for the job they say, 'We had a feeling about this particular person.' When I have heard about this 'feeling' I'm tempted to suggest that they take an aspirin and lie-down for a while—the feeling will pass. List Two is the 'likeability' list. The person who impresses most in both the competency and the likeability areas will be the person who gets the job.

One of the first interviews which I sat in on was at a pump manufacturing company which was looking for an engineer. As we went through the interviews it became clear to me that one of the applicants was outstanding on the competency factors. At the end of the interviews the employer asked my opinion, and I replied, 'No contest surely; one of the applicants is outstanding.' The employer agreed that one of the applicants was outstanding, but then declared that he had chosen somebody else.

'In one breath you agree that one was outstanding, and in the next you say you're choosing someone else. Why?'

'Because I think I can work with the person I have chosen.'

Many times since I've heard this sentiment expressed as a justification for choosing someone. What has happened is that the likeability factors are considered more important than the competency factors.

The only objective part of the interview process is the short-listing. Once an interview is begun we are in the realm of subjective decision-making. If all the applicants are much the same on the objective factors, then the only way of deciding between them is on the basis of the subjective, or likeability, factors. The important point to remember is that **if you get an interview you can assume you have enough competency factors for the job, but you will still have to work hard at demonstrating wisdom and likeability at the interview.**

Of course we are talking about 'likeable' in the work context: 'I would like to work with that person' or 'That person would fit in here'. After all, people who work full time spend more time at work than anywhere else, except, perhaps, in bed. It's no surprise that interviewers are very choosy about the person with whom they want to spend their time at work. Also, as you get older, the workplace becomes your main source of new friends, so interviewers have an even greater incentive to employ people with whom they feel comfortable. Work does have a social function, which the 'new right' economists, who talk about efficiency and productivity, sometimes lose track of.

However, there are some sound economic reasons why the likeability factor is so important. Many of us have had the experience of working with someone who is so hard to get on with that they damage the efficiency and productivity of the whole workplace.

This person may be the most qualified, skilled, experienced and knowledgeable in the job, but that is irrelevant if we can't work with him.

The relative importance of the likeability factor is directly related to how closely you will be working with the person doing the interviewing. If I am the personnel officer and I am interviewing someone whom I will hardly ever see again after this interview, then I am likely to pay as much attention to the competency as the likeability factors. On the other hand, if this is a small workplace and the person who gets the job will be working closely with me for the next few years, then likeability becomes much more important.

If you are going through an employment consultant before seeing an employer, you should be aware that consultants are much better at sticking to the competency factors. Why? Because they don't have to work with you. It is only with the employer that the likeability factor becomes crucial. Those consultants who recognise the importance of likeability may refer to what they call the PLU factor. These initials stand for People Like Us, a term which can be considered offensive.

Likeability is so important that it's worth exploring further. What sort of person do you like? What personal qualities do you find attractive? Suppose you are at a party. You meet eight new people and have short conversations with each. The next day you are shown a photograph of each person and asked your opinion of them. No doubt you would like some and dislike others. Why?

This is also a question which I pose to many groups which I coach, and the list they come up with usually looks more or less like this:

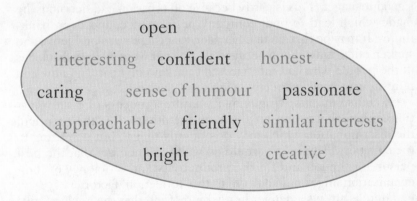

If we ask employers the same question, they are likely to come up with:

appeararance   enthusiasm   personality

communication   stability

Put the two together, and you have quite an imposing list. Most people preparing for an interview, if they prepare at all, tend naturally to concentrate on the factors in List One, omitting wisdom, insight and understanding, and do very little work on the combined factors in List Two, other than perhaps working on appearance. Whoever heard of someone who practised demonstrating a sense of humour for an interview? Anyone coached by me would include it in their preparation.

Another factor which is very influential at interviews is the 'reflection' factor. Most of us tend to be attracted to people we see as being like ourselves. Even if it is subconscious, we tend to favour people with the same backgrounds that we have, including race, colour, gender, socio-economic status, etc. The power of this reflection factor explains some of the illegal discrimination that can take place at interviews. While there is some malicious and deliberate discrimination, most illegal discrimination is not intended, but is subconscious and inadvertent.

The danger to employers who select staff in the same way that they select their friends, choosing people who are the most like themselves, is that they miss out on the benefits which diversity of views can bring to any situation. Indeed, in enlightened organisation, the 'ability to manage diversity' is now considered a characteristic of a good manager. This is partly because on occasion bad decisions are made which lead to poor company performance, and even bankruptcy. It may be that no-one has seen that there were problems, and spoken out against them, because all the staff were essentially clones of the people who had interviewed them: no diversity, no new and refreshing or vitally corrective views.

Of course interviewing is by its nature a process of discrimination: one person is chosen above all the others. It is the nature of the discrimination which may be not only illegal, but damaging to the company. Employers would do well to remember that the best person for the job and for the productivity and efficiency of their organisation might not conform to the 'reflection' factor.

There is always a danger in my kind of job that the advice I give may be taken to an extreme, and become counter-productive during an interview. Consider what happens if the following factors are taken too far:

open------>talkative
confident------>conceited
enthusiastic------>immature
sense of humour------>frivolous

We like people who are confident and open, but dislike those who are conceited and too talkative.

Clearly, the aim is to strike the right balance. If I were to choose, I would err on the side of under-doing rather than over-doing. I would rather hint at a sense of humour than appear a clown. I would rather be seen as thougthful than a blabbermouth.

To sum up this chapter, interviews are successful for those who can show that they are competent and at the same time that they are likeable. If all the applicants interviewed have a fairly even level of competence, what becomes crucial is how their ability is presented.

I was explaining this to a group of scientists who faced redundancy; their employer had hired me to coach them about how to find other work. One said angrily, 'Philip, this is unfair! We are scientists; we shouldn't be judged by these subjective factors. Scientists are not known for their ability to communicate or for their sense of humour, and what's more, these are irrelevant to our work.'

Although I agree that it is unfair, the fact remains that if I had a choice between two scientists with similar claims to a position, I would choose the one I'd most like to work with. If it is true that most scientists lack communication skills and humour—and I'm sure that many other scientists would disagree about this—then at least they're competing against others with similar qualities, and those who work to overcome the problem will do best.

In the following chapters we will look at how to present yourself at interviews, keeping in mind the need to demonstrate a balance between likeability and competency. I'll end this discussion of how the interviewer sees things with a quote from the personnel officer of a large organisation, who wants to remain anonymous: '*In my organisation we have an extensive and expensive process for choosing new staff. We advertise, we short-list, then we award a relative loading to each of the selection criteria. One question is then devised to "test" each of the selection criteria in turn. An equation is then formulated to compare the scores and consequently the relative merit of each applicant. When we have finished this laborious process we have a gut feeling about who we want to see in the job and we offer it to them.*'

Chapter 2

GETTING THE MIND-SET RIGHT

I remember an interview I helped to conduct as one of a panel of three for a mid-level supervisor's position in a large telecommunications organisation. The person in front of us was Kevin, a personable, middle-aged man whose background and experience made him eminently suitable for the position.

The position was only open to those already in the company, so I knew Kevin well. At least, I thought I did; the Kevin in front of me I did not recognise. He was nervous; he was so nervous, that his facial expressions, his movements and the tone of his voice were foreign to me. His agitation made me and my fellow panel members uncomfortable.

We had decided that after the small talk with each applicant at the start of the interview we would ask a few straightforward technical questions. This would not only give each applicant a chance early in the interview to demonstrate their knowledge but would also allow each person to settle down, feel more at ease, and thus respond better to the more difficult questions to follow. We were a nice, thoughtful panel. I am well aware that not all people who conduct interviews are as thoughtful.

We asked Kevin a straightforward question. He knew the answer, we knew that he knew the answer, he knew that we knew he knew the answer, which was 'three metres'. Kevin was so relieved that he knew the answer, that he promptly forgot it. The look of relief on his face was quickly replaced by a look of horror. He was a victim of the dreaded mental block.

He asked for the question to be repeated. 'I know it. I know it', he murmured to himself. 'What is it again? It's on the tip of my tongue! Don't tell me', he laboured. By this stage Kevin could not look at any of us, and he shielded his eyes with one hand. 'Don't tell me, don't tell me', he continued, but this time his other hand started beckoning towards us. The voice was saying 'don't tell me' but the body language was saying 'tell me, tell me, for goodness' sake, tell me!'

Sound familiar? Most of us have an interview horror story. It is not uncommon for someone at an interview to suffer from a mental block. I have seen people in such a state that they stumble over their own name.

The rest of Kevin's interview was poor. He didn't recover from the bad start, and we didn't promote him. We were not able to promote him even though our personal knowledge of him told us he was more than capable of doing the job in question.

Bureaucratic? Maybe, but we knew that all the applicants were capable of doing the job and we had only one vacant position. If we had allowed personal knowledge to influence the outcome we would have been open to charges of favouritism or nepotism. Besides, when I tried to put up a case for Kevin, another panel member pointed out that communication skills were part of the selection criteria and Kevin had certainly not demonstrated any.

I spoke to Kevin a few days after the interview. 'What happened to you in there?' Kevin turned on me angrily: 'You don't understand. I hate interviews. I hate interviews!'

I have lost count of the number of times I have heard that phrase. Many people hate interviews, and those who don't, usually dislike them or are at least made uncomfortable by them. When was the last time you heard someone say, 'Oh joy! I have an interview next week. I can hardly wait!'? Personally, I have a good record at interviews, but I still feel some anxiety beforehand.

In addition to Kevin we interviewed six applicants. The chances were that all of them either hated, disliked or were made uncomfortable by interviews. But no one else allowed this to hinder their performance the way that Kevin did.

To gather more information about why people hate interviews I armed myself with a clipboard and went out one Saturday to my local shopping centre. I asked dozens of people at random their thoughts on interviews, and if they disliked interviews, why. Here are some of the more interesting and printable responses:

Angela, a 28-year-old research officer:

> *'I hate interviews because you have to evaluate yourself in order to put forward your strengths and weaknesses. It is not pleasant having to confront your weaknesses.'*

This was in part supported by Leslie, a 36-year-old production worker:

> *'... because I'm not perfect and they are always looking for someone who is.'*

Bridget, a 23-year-old printing assistant, hates interviews because:

> *'I hate people questioning my integrity, particularly when I'm not sure of theirs.'*

James, 53 years old, with qualifications in accountancy:

> *'Most of the time I go for interviews I know more than the interviewers, and I hate that. Sometimes I think if life was fairer I would be interviewing them.'*

Gerard, a 26-year-old mechanic, introduced job skills versus interview technique into the picture:

> *'In mechanics, it should be how good you are, how well you can fix something. Mechanics don't do a lot of talking to people, but interviews are just talking to people. They should just get you to fix something or put you on and try you out. What's the point of having trades papers if employers still question you?'*

Sylvie, a 42-year-old kitchen worker:

> *'I hate interviews because I don't have a silver spoon in my mouth and I miss out to those who do.'*

Stephen, a 56-year-old senior manager:

> *'At my level it seems that there is always a hidden agenda. They are always looking for something extra that they never mention. It's usually an attitudinal thing. Sometimes they might want someone who has a good standing with the unions, another time they might want someone who can take the unions on, but they never say up front. It's like they don't believe someone can have both these attributes depending on the situation. So you end up trying to second-guess what they are looking for. I try not to make the same mistakes myself when I am interviewing.'*

Perhaps the most succinct response came from 56-year-old Joseph, a telecommunications worker:

> *'Interviews are bullshit. The one who bullshits the best gets the job. I can bullshit with the best of them but I don't like having to do it.'*

Two responses occurred time and time again:

> *'I dislike interviews because I'm not good at them and I don't get the job.'*
> *'I dislike interviews because I don't like people who don't know me, passing judgement on my ability.'*

Very few people said they liked interviews. The people who

did, fell into two categories: they had a history of being successful at interviews, or their skills were in such demand that their interview performance was not a factor in gaining work. One who liked interviews was 37-year-old Darryl, who was in real estate. Darryl said he had spent a large amount of money on a personal development course, which, among other things, had taught him to see interviews as 'windows of opportunity'.

In my experience there are three main reasons why people dislike interviews:

1. The fear of failure

Interviews are competitions and, as in all competitions, there are winners and losers. Few people enjoy losing, especially when they are not sure why they lost. In sport, if you play badly and get beaten by someone who plays better, you can console yourself in this knowledge. You are probably aware of where you went wrong and can work on your weaknesses to improve your chances next time. In an interview it is the grey areas, the uncertainty about your own performance and how and where to try harder, that cause problems.

Failure at an interview can be devastating, not only damaging your self-esteem, but also having direct financial repercussions, particularly if you have a mortgage or a car to keep on the road. In many cases our dislike of interviews is in direct proportion to how much we want/need the job.

2. Dislike of 'performing'

It seems that there are more introverts in the world than extroverts. We have already noted that interviews are a performance and that not everyone likes to perform. Over the years newspaper polls have asked people what they fear most. Public speaking often ranks number one. Apparently some people prefer spiders, snakes, rats or mice, even death to public speaking! A job interview is a form of public speaking—a very intimate form. There is also the problem of having to say nice things about ourselves publicly, which many of us dislike. And the very fact that we have to perform, put on an act, before we can get ahead or earn a living makes many people indignant.

3. The problem of honesty

Honesty in an interview is a double-edged sword. Most of us do not like to 'creatively shape' our work histories so as to be competitive at an interview and yet we feel compelled to exaggerate. At the same time we question whether or not the interviewers are honest. Are they really looking for someone? Has someone got their name on the job already? Has someone been given the questions before the interview? If I get the job will it be as good as they are making it out to be?

At some stage in the interview a question may be asked that may make you think, 'I know what they want to hear and I know what the truth is, and the two are not the same.' Do you tell them what they want to hear and not sleep tonight because you have told a lie, or do you tell them the truth and not sleep because you've missed out on the job you wanted? It's not an enjoyable choice.

Despite the common dislike of interviews, there are people who believe that although they hate interviews, all around are others who love them. What a nonsense this is! Imagine being told, 'You can have this job with or without an interview; which would you prefer?'

Dislike of interviews affects job-seekers in three main ways:

1. Over-trying

Many people are so afraid of not knowing an answer at an interview that they study, study, study until they are overloaded with information. They don't stop to consider how they will present this information. The result is they offer a mish-mash of facts that often do not flow together, or may not even be relevant to the question asked. It is important to remember that being able to state facts is completely different from being able to demonstrate understanding and wisdom.

Most interviewers are aware that people who over-try have at least made an effort to interview well, and although it is an interview technique problem, it is the easiest to forgive. But of course this doesn't mean that you can have this problem and be competitive against someone who presents the information in a more orderly, engaging way.

2. Under-trying

> *'I can live with failing the interview if I don't try in the first place!'*

> *'If I didn't get the job because I didn't study, because I didn't dress right, because I didn't appear enthusiastic, because I had a hangover and wasn't at my best, then people I know will understand and it won't reflect as badly on me as a person.'*

Under-trying is a very common form of poor interview technique. The saddest and most disappointing of all interviews to witness is when the job-seeker builds in an excuse to soften the hurt of failure, and often causes interviewers to wonder why the person bothered to come in the first place. This under-trying is not necessarily the result of a conscious decision; most often it is subconscious. Don't be the person who under-tries: you will be wasting your time and the time of others.

Occasionally a sympathetic interviewer will include an applicant who under-tried at the first interview in a second round of interviews. It is astonishing how much better the person usually does at the second interview. The feeling that they have a chance and are being taken seriously despite their built-in excuse bolsters confidence and they put more effort into their second interview preparation. If the applicant had the ability to try harder all along, then this should have been reflected in the first interview.

3. Nervousness

This unfortunate form of poor interview technique manifests itself in many ways, most commonly are 'umms and ahs'. Other indications of nervousness are rambling on and on in the vain hope that if you talk long enough you must say the right thing at some stage, continual one word answers, repeatedly asking the interviewers to clarify the question and, in extreme cases, mental blocks.

This type of interview is also painful for the interviewers and is sometimes referred to as 'pulling teeth', since each answer has to be extracted with effort. The good news is that nervousness is the easiest poor interview technique to remedy.

It should be apparent by now that the first lesson to learn in improving interview technique is that, for many reasons, it is natural to dislike interviews. The sooner you accept this and realise it is the same for everyone, the better off you will be. Instead of dwelling on the negatives of the situation, put your energy into considering the interview in as positive a light as you can, while trying to avoid the pitfalls that anxiety about the interview can cause. Interviews are not real life, they are a game. If you cannot muster real enthusiasm for them, at least practise faking it.

It should boost your confidence to know that the majority of people at all levels, from managers to labourers, interview very poorly. If eight people are interviewed the chances are that all eight will be poor. As a result, many decisions are made on a comparative basis: the least worst will get the job. However, in this book I will be describing the highest standard of interview possible. Even if you fall short of that standard you should still do better than most interviewees.

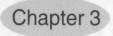

Chapter 3

PREPARATION

People who are regularly on interview panels soon realise that they will be interviewing the same people over and over again. These are people who would apply for a position, miss out, and apply again next time a vacancy occurs either for the same or a different position. These people usually already work for the organisation and are applying for internal promotions, but some are persistent applicants from outside the organisation. I have interviewed some people four times for the one position, and others as many as seven or eight times for different positions.

Being unsuccessful on any one occasion is understandable; it could be an off day, the competition might be too strong, or you could just be caught out being too ambitious. Being unsuccessful on two or more occasions is acceptable as long as you are improving each time. Being unsuccessful on a number of occasions and not improving is completely unacceptable, yet many people perform poorly time and time again—from employer to employer, from job to job.

It is very frustrating to ask someone a question, the same question you asked at a similar interview two months earlier, and hear them answer in the same poor way that they did before. If it didn't work well the first time, why would it on any subsequent occasion?

If you were learning to play tennis you would not expect to pick up a racquet and start winning matches on day one. There would be many things you would have to learn: forehand, backhand, lobs, serves, volleys, etc. You would not expect to be an overnight champion, but would take lessons and would practise. Natural ability may take you so far but to become competitive you need to practise. After a while you would sort out which parts of the game were your strengths and which your weaknesses. You would take extra tuition and focus your practice on your weaknesses. Then you might expect to start winning a few games.

Job interviews are no different. Before achieving success you have to work out the broad range of skills necessary, identify which are your strengths and weaknesses and then work on the weaknesses with assistance and practice.

Some interviewees who do prepare are not sure how best to direct their energies. One of the most common trap is to believe that the applicant who can store and recall the most information will get the job, but this is rarely the case. I have watched people preparing for interviews by writing down pages of facts, tables and data, and then trying to learn them by rote. In the end they only succeed in over-trying.

Job interviews are not merely tests of memory. Information is important, but it is not all-important. Remember that if thirty people apply for a position and eight people are interviewed after efficient short-listing, all eight will have similar information. If information was the primary basis for selection and each applicant passed on the same information, the interviewers would be no closer to making a decision after the interviews than they were before.

Of course this rarely happens. Different people present the same information in different ways. This very important point is overlooked by many applicants. It is not just having the required information, it is the way in which the information is presented that distinguishes between applicants. The essential difference is one of approach.

Good interviewees see interviews as an opportunity to sell themselves for the position. As an interviewee you are not in the driver's seat, but nor should you be merely a passenger.

This emphasis on 'selling' at interview may seem obvious, but it is very difficult for a lot of people. Many people are uncomfortable with the thought of selling themselves, or of thinking of themselves as a commodity that has to be sold. If you are the sort of person who is in this category then the mention of selling may lead to thoughts of used car or insurance salespeople, or politicians, because popular culture, perhaps unfairly, denigrates these occupations.

In preparing for an interview you must dismiss any thoughts that selling yourself is in some way sleazy or unethical. In a job interview you and your product are one and the same thing. Instead, think of the nicest salesperson you know, and let this person be your model. Keeping your mind on using interview questions to their best possible benefit for you, will help give a better focus to your preparation.

Preparation for an interview should involve two basic aspects:

1. Determining the

words

that you are going to say.

2. Working on the

presentation

of those words

The following chapters will help you in these areas.

Once you have prepared the words and the presentation, you should do a number of mock interviews. Start by asking yourself questions out loud and then answering to the best of your ability. Be sure to include details such as body language, inflection and gestures. Once you are happy with the results find someone to listen to you and comment on your presentation. The best person to help with a mock interview is someone who understands the position you are applying for, but don't discount the value of running through an interview with a partner, friend or neighbour, even if they don't know all the details of the job.

If you don't like interviews you probably won't like mock interviews either, but you have to overcome this aversion. Mock interviews are a very important part of preparation, and there is no substitute for them. A set of words that sounds fine to you may sound unclear to someone else. Never forget that the interview is a performance, and no actors, not even the world's best, will perform without a rehearsal. Why assume you can? Thinking that you do not have to go through some mock interviews is essentially conceited, and may well be your undoing.

Thorough preparation is vital to a good interview performance, and there are no shortcuts available. People who prepare well interview well; people who do not prepare well do not interview well. It's as simple as that.

WRITTEN APPLICATIONS

Although I am concentrating on the interview process, it would be remiss not to mention one of the main ways of gaining an interview: written applications. It may seem strange that this chapter comes after the chapter on interview preparation, not before, but I have done this for two reasons.

1. The preparation for a written application and an interview should be similar. For this reason the points covered in the previous chapter are also relevant to preparing written applications.

2. The most common mistake made in written applications is the same as the most common mistake made at interviews. Interviewees who see questions as requests for information only, and earnestly believe that is all the interviewer requires, are the same applicants who provide résumés that are only lists of information or historical accounts of their past.

The best approach when preparing written applications and résumés is this: pretend you are a shop-keeper and that the résumé and covering letter are your shop windows. With shoppers walking past, what will entice them to come inside and buy? Of course you would put all your best goods on display in the window, in the most attractive possible way.

After reading your application will the employer come inside and buy: invite you to an interview? Not if the most attractive goods are under lock and key in a safe in the cellar, and can only be found by someone who is prepared to go looking for them.

This is why I am critical of résumés which are merely lists of information. Such lists show little or no wisdom, insight and understanding, much less the disposition, personality or beliefs of the applicant. When an employer may read over a hundred applications, lists start to look amazingly similar or even worse, boring.

Over recent years, job applicants have become aware of the need for their written applications to stand out. Many have tried to improve their presentation, and the standard of applications has risen dramatically.

The first improvement was in the professionalism of presentation. The advent of home computers and printers gave more people access to new technology and soon applications tapped out on a portable typewriter gave way to printed presentations. When most job-seekers presented their applications this way, those who wanted to stay ahead in the 'outstanding application' race moved to using a laser printer, with its even greater level of professional presentation. Again this advantage was short lived as laser-printed applications became fairly standard. Desk-top publishing then came into vogue, and applications which had borders, tables, different typefaces, fancy headings and foot and header notes became commonplace.

The next stage was to use coloured paper for résumés, or at least their first page, the idea being that they would stand out from the sea of white. This too became standard, so that opening a group of applications now reveals a kaleidoscope of colour. The latest trend is as bold as it will be short lived: job applicants are using coloured graphics and even cartoon characters crowing such things as, 'If you want to read the résumé of someone energetic, efficient and creative then read on ...'. Applications presented in this way certainly stand out at first, but they lose all impact and even start looking silly if half a dozen similar applications are received. In fact, standing out by way of presentation has gone about as far as it can without becoming ridiculous.

Some applicants include a personal photograph. If you are applying for a position which involves public contact and that therefore personal appearance and grooming are important, by all means include a photograph. If you are not applying for a position involving public contact, however, a photograph of yourself is probably superfluous and may be regarded as gimmicky.

With all this competition, how do you make sure your application will be read, and will gain you an interview? If you are getting an interview less than once in every three applications then serious consideration should be given to revamping your résumé. I write this on a day when I have spoken to someone who has applied for 120 positions and sent off the same résumé 120 times, to be granted the grand total of two interviews. Why did they continue to send out the same résumé when it was so spectacularly unsuccessful? Because they did not know any better, as simple as that.

There is no magic formula for written applications; there will always be an aspect of 'submit and hope'. However, it is important to your self-esteem that your written applications are the best you are able to achieve.

Let's take the real example of one of my clients, whom I will call Alice Smith. Alice was facing retrenchment because the company she worked for was being taken over by another company and there was much talk of restructuring. Alice had broad administrative skills and had recently been working as a secretary and personal assistant. When she first saw me she was applying for the position described in the following advertisement.

PERSONAL ASSISTANT

Attractive Salary Package

This challenging and interesting position has become vacant as the result of an internal promotion. The new appointee will complement the activities and responsibilities of a Company Director. This will include working with a key executive, liaison within the wider organisation as well as externally with members of industry and commerce, customers and the public sector. The role will include substantial organisational and secretarial responsibilities. There will be an emphasis on co-ordinating functions, while maintaining a watching brief in respect of overall internal relations, planning and scheduling.

The successful applicant will have had demonstrable experience as a Senior PA/Secretary. Excellent communication and interpersonal skills are essential, as is competency in Word for Windows. Some exposure to Excel and other PC software would be an advantage. Shorthand and dictaphone skills are also required. Further, the appointee will be able to work flexible hours, accept responsibility and be service and results oriented.

We are able to offer the successful candidate excellent long-term career prospects. This position should therefore appeal to an outgoing, disciplined and intelligent professional who is seeking the opportunity to complement a close knit and successful team.

Initial telephone enquiries are welcome on 3366 4411. Applications should be sent to John Gomez, Personnel Officer, Acme Corp, 6 Industry Court, Brownsville, Qld 4576. Quote position number 1243. Applications close Wednesday, 19 January 1997.

Apart from the names, this is a copy of the real advertisement. Let us see how Alice responded.

Covering Letters

First of all, she composed a covering letter. Many job applicants view the covering letter as a waste of paper. It is not unusual to see covering letters with this content (the lay-out of the letter would be more professional):

Mr John Gomez
Personnel Officer
Acme Corp
6 Industry Drive
Brownsville
Qld 4567

Dear Mr Gomez

I wish to apply for the position of Personal Assistant (your reference position number 1243) as advertised in the Daily Informer on 3/1/97. For your consideration I have enclosed a copy of my résumé. I look forward to hearing from you soon. I am available for interview any time at your convenience.

Yours sincerely

Alice Smith

The résumé that follows this covering letter will undoubtedly be a list of information. The problem with this covering letter is that it wastes an opportunity to sell Alice for the position.

Alice's letter was not quite as bare as this example; hers was a more common type:

Dear Mr Gomez
I wish to apply for the position
of Personal Assistant (your
reference position number 1243)
as advertised in the Daily
Informer on 3/1/97.

For your consideration I have
enclosed a copy of my résumé. I
believe that my résumé will
demonstrate that I have the
complete range of skills and
experience to be able to achieve
in the advertised position.

Furthermore I believe that Acme
Corp is a good, sound, ethical
company and that I could make a
contribution to its ongoing
competitiveness.

I look forward to hearing from
you soon. I am available for
interview any time at your
convenience.

Yours sincerely

Alice Smith

This is a better letter, although not a great deal better. It is warmer in its tone and it is more interesting and pleasant to read. Other than this, however, it does little more than again direct the reader to the résumé.

The advertisement encourages people to ring with any enquiries but Alice chose not to take advantage of this offer because she felt the advertisement was straightforward and self-explanatory and she didn't know what else to ask about. After talking to me, Alice rang and asked a range of questions about the structure of the company, where the advertised position fitted into the company, the company's products and its markets. This information was included in her covering letter and later referred to at interview. Here is the letter that Alice finally submitted, which was successful in gaining her an interview.

Dear Mr Gomez

I wish to apply for the position of Personal Assistant (your reference position number 1243) as advertised in the Daily Informer on 3/1/97.

For your consideration I have enclosed a copy of my résumé. I believe that my résumé will demonstrate that I have the complete range of skills and experience to be able to achieve in the advertised position including the communication and computer skills mentioned. It is harder in a résumé to demonstrate the personal qualities and beliefs that I have which are also necessary to be a good Personal Assistant (PA).

Manufacturing industry is going through a period of significant change and it is important that senior managers are able to devote their energies to ensuring that gains result from this change. I believe that PAs should assist in this process by freeing senior managers to devote time to the serious issues while the PA takes care of the more peripheral issues.

To do this successfully the PA must be able to develop a relationship with a Senior Manager built on understanding, trust and the ability to keep confidences. It is the quality of this relationship which often is as much the measure of the efficiency of a PA as the technical skills.

A good PA also has a broad understanding of the structures of the company, the industry in general, the markets for the company products and influencing factors on those markets.

I understand the importance of a good PA and I am sure that my referees will attest to my good nature and my personal qualities as well as my skills and experience. This is why I am applying for this position.

I look forward to hearing from you soon. I am available for interview any time at your convenience.

Yours sincerely

Alice Smith

Alice has shown some understanding of the role of a PA and its importance. She has also directly raised the issue of the relationship of the PA and the executive, a relationship vital to productivity and efficiency, and undoubtedly the key unstated selection criterion. Pointing this out in her covering letter is likely to have struck a favourable chord with the person reading it. Alice has also shown insight into the changes taking place within manufacturing industry at this time. Given that her résumé continued the good impression that her covering letter created, it is not surprising that she was short-listed.

Some employers prefer a covering letter to be handwritten, in the belief that the handwriting offers an insight into the applicant's character. While this view is not universal, it is worth considering a handwritten application if you have neat, easy-to-read writing.

Many people have the mistaken belief that covering letters should be restricted to one page. There is no such restriction. Covering letters can be too long, but also too short. I have seen letters four pages long methodically addressing selection criteria with not a word out of place. I have also seen covering letters of two pages with so much waffle in them that they are a page too long. A covering letter should be just long enough to include all the points necessary to gain you an interview.

Of course there are some employers who do not read covering letters, who habitually screw them up and throw them away, relying solely on the résumé. In such a case there is no harm done; Alice will gain an interview or not solely on her résumé.

The other case in which a covering letter may not make an impact is when the application is sent to an employment agency and not directly to an employer. Employment consultants tend to concentrate more on the details of the résumé alone.

Résumés

As you can tell I am in the habit of using the word 'résumé' to refer to the sheets of information giving personal details, skills and experience. Other people call it a 'curriculum vitae' (which is Latin for 'life history'), often abbreviated to CV, or their 'biodata'. It is a matter of personal choice which of these you use, although for positions in the scientific or academic fields, 'curriculum vitae' is the common term.

The most common problem with the way that many people present their résumés is that they are bland, dry lists of information which are not reader-friendly. They are usually historical in nature, concentrating solely on what has been done without looking to what might be done in the future. Employers often have to seek out the part of the résumé which is relevant to the job in question. This is annoying. There is no reason why a résumé should not be easy to read and interesting.

Another common fault is that many people have only the one résumé and consider it an unchangeable document. They say such things as, 'This is my résumé' or, 'I have had my résumé professionally written', implying that this is the only way information about themselves can be presented. Unless you are applying for exactly the same position each time, there should be no such thing as a fixed résumé.

Résumés need to be tailored, and sometimes should even undergo major structural change, as you apply for different jobs. For example, if you feel that you may not receive an interview because you are over-qualified for a job, don't put all your qualifications into your résumé. This is not illegal or even immoral, it is simply presenting the information you believe is relevant to the job in question.

Other alterations that you may wish to consider are: giving a different perspective to previous positions by changing their titles (e.g. a 'sales clerk' can become a 'customer service operator', or in a small store, an 'assistant manager'), putting a different emphasis on the responsibilities of previous positions to bring them more obviously into line with the position applied for. If you do this you might have to get the agreement of former referees whom you are using again.

Understand that to use only the one résumé is to apply what I call the 'shotgun' approach, that is, to send the one résumé off to as many employers as possible in the hope that it is exactly what one of them is looking for. There have been times when this approach has been acceptable and indeed successful; those times are not now. Unless you possess skills and experience in short supply and heavy demand the shotgun approach does not work well. Employers like to think that their job and their organisation may hold some specific attraction for you.

The most effective résumé is the one which appears to easily match the specific needs of the job. This is why I am critical of the job seeker support companies that have sprung up offering to produce professionally presented résumés for a fee. While the fee may be quite reasonable for one résumé, if several résumés with different approaches are needed, it can get quite expensive. This expense pushes people to use the one résumé for all applications which lowers employment chances rather than enhancing them.

Let's look at Alice Smith's standard résumé as she first showed it to me:

RÉSUMÉ

NAME: Alice Smith

ADDRESS: 1 Green Street,
                             Brownsville, Qld 4567

TELEPHONE: 3333 2222

PERSONAL DETAILS:

Date of Birth: 29/9/59

Health: Good

Interests: . Reading
                             . Current Affairs
                             . Softball
                             . Italian Culture

DEMONSTRATED ABILITIES:

Secretarial Skills: . Keyboard—60 wpm
                             . Shorthand—80 wpm
                             . Dictaphone
                             . Organisational Abilities

Accounting Skills: . Maintained records of
                               accounts
                               receivable/payable and
                               computer payroll.
                             . Assisted in preparation of
                               monthly departmental
                               accounts and budget.

Computing Skills: . DOS, Word Perfect 5.1,
                               Word for Windows, Lotus
                               123, Excel

Administrative Skills: . Minute Secretary to
                               various committees and
                               subcommittees.

	.	Drafted a set of Finance Guidelines.
	.	Assisted in several ongoing research projects.
	.	Personnel systems including leave, pay and allowances.
Communication Skills:	.	Liaised with management, staff, customers and various government departments.
	.	Answered written and personal enquiries and complaints from staff, customers and suppliers.
	.	Interviewed respondents for market research as part of project.

EDUCATION:

1972	High School Diploma Brownsville Secondary College
1973–74	Certificate of Secretarial Studies Brownsville Secretarial College
1985	Introduction to Computers
1986	Word Processing—Beginners Word Processing—Intermediate Word Processing—Advanced
1987	Spreadsheets—Beginners
1988	Spreadsheets—Intermediate
1990–91	Introduction to Marketing

EMPLOYMENT:

1991–current   Personal Assistant
                      Ace Manufacturing

1988–1991   Secretary
                      Ace Manufacturing
                      Marketing Section

1984–1988   Personnel Clerk
                      City of Brownsville

1979–1984   Accounts Clerk
                      City of Brownsville

1975–1979   Junior Clerk/Clerk
                      Style Fabrics

REFEREES:

Business: Milo Janowski
                      Marketing Manager
                      Ace Manufacturing
                      Tel: 3333 8791

                      Sally Johanssen
                      City Manager
                      Newtown (ex Brownsville)
                      Tel: 3482 7132

Personal: Georgina Harrow
                      President
                      Brownsville Softball Club
                      Tel: 3484 9343

This is not a bad résumé by any comparative standard; that is, the content of most résumés look similar to Alice's. The résumé was very professional in its appearance and had a coloured title page which only had 'RÉSUMÉ—ALICE SMITH' on it in large type. Alice had made some decisions about format: she had decided to put abilities first and her work history second, rather than the other way around or combining the two. The problem I had with Alice's résumé was that it was a dry, untailored list of information that undersold Alice for the job. Was it correct? Yes. Was it appealing? No, not really.

Another minor criticism I had with the résumé was Alice's decision to put her personal details on the first page. If we go back to the shop window analogy we have to think position, position, position. It is not impossible but highly unlikely that someone would give Alice an interview because she was interested in Italian culture or played softball. Use the front page to display the reasons why you should be granted an interview.

The following is the résumé that Alice eventually used; she was much happier with this than with her original. We retained the coloured title sheet, and the next sheet looked like this:

PRÉCIS OF CRITICAL SKILLS RELEVANT TO PERSONAL ASSISTANT ACME CORP

- ALICE SMITH -

EXPERIENCE:
- 6 years as Personal Assistant to Senior Manager
- 3 years as Senior Secretary manufacturing environment
- 12 years broad experience in other administrative roles— personnel and accounts

SKILLS:
- Organisational abilities
- Keyboard—60 wpm
- Shorthand—80 wpm
- Dictaphone
- DOS, Word Perfect 5.1, Word for Windows, Lotus 123, Excel

PERSONAL QUALITIES: It would be easy to provide a long list of adjectives to try to impress you, but basically I am skilled, reliable, easy to get on with and take an interest and pride in my work.

This précis at the beginning is the easiest way to show that the information is specifically written with Acme Corp in mind. It is also a good way of gaining the attention of someone wading through a sea of applications and making it easy for them. Alice's résumé continued on the next sheet:

RÉSUMÉ

- ALICE SMITH -

ADDRESS: 1 Green Street,
                      Brownsville, Qld 4567

TELEPHONE: 3333 2222

EXPERIENCE:

1991–current   **Personal Assistant**
                            Ace Manufacturing

Responsibilities: Working closely with and
                           taking direction from
                           Senior Manager
                           Marketing. Maintaining
                           all records and
                           correspondence files
                           incoming and outgoing.
                           Being a proxy at meetings.
                           Liaising on behalf of
                           Manager Marketing
                           internally and externally.
                           Organising diary entries
                           and arranging travel,
                           filtering calls—sorting out
                           the chaff from the wheat.

Reason for leaving: Company about to be taken over, causing uncertainty as to future tenure.

1988–1991 **Senior Secretary**
Ace Manufacturing

Responsibilities: Providing a full range of secretarial services to a group of managers on an 'as needs' basis. This work involved authoring of reports and correspondence for signature when necessary.

Reason for leaving: Promoted within the company. Approached to consider the position of Personal Assistant. The satisfaction of taking on extra responsibility.

1984–1988 **Personnel Clerk**
City of Brownsville

Responsibilities: Full range of personnel duties including leave records, pay and allowances, and administering and advising on personnel policies such as staff appraisal. Includes periods of higher responsibilities as Personnel Manager.

| Reason for leaving: | Seeking greater job satisfaction through full use of my skills. I had trained at secretarial college and I felt that I would lose these skills forever if I did not find a position that used them. Desire to return to work in private industry. |

1979–1984   **Accounts Clerk**
City of Brownsville

| Responsibilities: | Full range of accounts duties including receivable and payable. Maintaining records and assessing tax liability. |

| Reason for leaving: | Promotion to Personnel Section. While I enjoy working with figures I felt that I was better suited to working with people. |

1975–1979   **Junior Clerk/Clerk**
Style Fabrics

| Responsibilities: | First job after leaving secretarial college. I was considered too young to work as a secretary. Started out doing basic report typing and fetching lunches. Moved into stock control, inventories and customer orders. |

| Reason for leaving: | Advancement. Desire to vary work experience and work for a larger organisation. |

DEMONSTRATED ABILITIES:

PA/Secretarial Skills: Keyboard 60 wpm, Shorthand 80 wpm, dictaphone, organisational abilities. Ability to draft wide range of correspondence. Understanding of organisational objectives. All the skills you would expect from an experienced PA.

Accounting Skills: Maintained records of accounts receivable/payable and computer payroll. Assisted in preparation of monthly departmental accounts and budget. I have an understanding of ledgers and have done trial balances.

Computing Skills: DOS, Word Perfect 5.1, Word for Windows, Lotus 123, Excel

Administrative Skills:
. Minute Secretary to various committees and subcommittees.
. Drafted a set of Finance Guidelines.
. Assisted in several ongoing research projects.
. Personnel systems including leave, pay and allowances.

Communication Skills: . Liaised with management, staff, customers and various government departments.

. Answered written and personal enquiries and complaints from staff, customers and suppliers.

. Interviewed respondents for market research as part of project.

. Ability to run meetings.

EDUCATION:

1972	High School Diploma Brownsville Secondary College
1973–74	Certificate of Secretarial Studies Brownsville Secretarial College
1985	Introduction to Computers
1986	Word Processing—Beginners Word Processing—Intermediate Word Processing—Advanced
1987	Spreadsheets—Beginners
1988	Spreadsheets—Intermediate
1990–91	Introduction to Marketing
1975–1997	I have also attended numerous in-house training courses covering a wide range of topics.

As you can see, education has always been an ongoing concern to me. I like to keep learning, and I would happily learn any new skills which would assist me at Acme Corp.

PERSONAL DETAILS:

Date of Birth: 29/9/59

Health: Good

Interests: . Reading
                        . Current Affairs
                        . Softball
                        . Italian Culture

REFEREES:

Business: **Milo Janowski**
                            Marketing Manager
                            Ace Manufacturing
                            Tel: 3333 8791

                            Sally Johanssen
                            City Manager
                            Newtown (ex Brownsville)
                            Tel: 3482 7132

Personal: **Georgina Harrow**
                            President
                            Brownsville Softball Club
                            Tel: 3484 9343

I have spoken to each of these referees and they are
pleased to speak on my behalf. Please ring them if you
have any enquiries.

This is better than the original résumé for the job at Acme Corp. It
provides similar information to the original but it does so in a more
personal, comprehensive and accessible way. It remains in point
form but provides some insight into Alice and her thoughts rather
than being just a list of facts. It is more appealing.

Some of the items included in Alice's résumé were optional,
such as her date of birth and the reasons that she left previous positions. I would only include reasons for leaving previous positions if
such reasons were obviously justifiable and explicable.

If Alice didn't get the Acme Corp job and she was applying for
another position, then she should tailor her résumé to suit and it
would look quite different in many of its key aspects. Her précis of
critical skills might look like this:

PRÉCIS OF CRITICAL SKILLS RELEVANT TO PERSONNEL CLERK

JOHNSON AUTOMOTIVE

- ALICE SMITH -

EXPERIENCE: 13 years in personnel work, 6 years in manufacturing environment.

SKILLS: Full range of personnel work including leave records, pay and allowances (both manual and computer) and policy development and administration. Broad range of computer skills.

PERSONAL QUALITIES: It would be easy to provide a list of adjectives to try to impress you, but basically I am skilled, reliable, easy to get on with and take an interest and pride in my work.

Alice's last nine years at Ace Manufacturing are now no longer presented as secretarial/PA work but have been merged into personnel work. The résumé itself would have to be substantially changed to reflect this. She would make no mention of secretarial/PA work, other than secretarial school, and she would join the last two positions at Ace Manufacturing together and refer to them as 'administrator', including any personnel-related duties in the 'responsibilities' description. Personal assistants always have some personnel related duties so this would not be an outright fabrication. To be able to make these changes Alice would need the agreement of her referee from Ace Manufacturing. My experience is that most referees are understanding in this regard. If a referee is not prepared to assist, then look for another.

In summing up this chapter on written applications, you should remember the following points:

✔ written applications need to be well presented, but they do not need to be an art form

✔ the covering letter is an important tool and time should be devoted to it

✔ covering letters and résumés need to be tailored to suit each individual position

✔ written applications need to be accessible, engaging and appealing

✔ written applications should give some insight into your views and beliefs, and a list of adjectives under 'Personal Qualities' does not do this satisfactorily.

The most important point is that your written application has only one purpose: to get you an interview. It will be worth the time to see how many applications you may have submitted recently, compared with the number of interviews you have been granted.

Chapter 5

FINDING
THE WORDS

Your application and résumé have been successful and you have been granted an interview. Now you have to do the preparation. Many people ask, 'How do you work on the words you are going to use when you do not know the questions that will be asked?'

Of course you can't know exactly, but by carefully considering the selection criteria, by doing a little investigating, by learning from previous interviews, by using commonsense, you can, more often than not, gain some real insight into which questions will be asked.

In addition, there will be some points you will want to make at an interview, regardless of whether they fit neatly as the answer to a question, and these points need to be prepared. To see yourself as merely a passenger in the interview process is a tactical error which may prevent you from taking opportunities to manipulate the interview in your favour.

The first step in preparing the words is to investigate the selection criteria. Often, particularly in large organisations, the selection criteria are readily available and will be sent to you on request. If there are no written selection criteria, it is perfectly acceptable to ring and ask the appropriate person, 'What will you be looking for in the person who gets this position?'

Sometimes there are no written selection criteria because they are considered self-evident. In this case your own knowledge of the job, and commonsense, should guide you to the likely questions. Sometimes, if the position has appeared in a large block advertisement in a newspaper, sufficient selection criteria are indicated within the advertisement. A request to the organisation may be directed back to the advertisement. Therefore, do not take the advertisement lightly; careful analysis should always take place. If the advertisement asks for certain skills and qualities it is a fair guess that some questions will focus on these skills or qualities, even if the question is as broad as 'what do you have to offer?'.

My experience is that consultants or agencies are better than employers at wording advertisements to indicate what qualities are needed in the job.

Just as most jobs have written selection criteria, most jobs also have unwritten selection criteria which are as important, if not more important, than the selection criteria. Many interviewees tackle the written selection criteria, but fewer understand the unwritten criteria. I will demonstrate how to do this in the section 'Questions and Answers'.

Once you have some idea of the selection criteria the next thing to do is to frame some questions. What would you ask if you were interviewing? What have you been asked at previous interviews? Later in this book I will take a look at common question types.

Another way to help in preparing for questions is to visit the workplace.

Workplace Visits

I strongly recommend visiting the place of work where you have applied for a position. The best way to do this is openly, as a candidate for a position:

> *'I have been granted an interview for a position at your company. My interview is next Friday and as I will be in the area today I was wondering if I could come in for a few minutes and have a look around and ask a few questions to help me in my interview preparation?'*

Always ring first and make an appointment, never just turn up. In making the appointment speak to the person who contacted you about the interview. This is to protect yourself on those rare occasions when someone is about to be replaced but does not yet know it. It is embarrassing all round to ring someone and tell them you are to be interviewed for their job when they did not know they were to be replaced.

For some reason many people have the idea that it is rude to visit a workplace before you are interviewed for a position there. It is not rude; it is showing interest. In my experience it is uncommon for these requests to be refused and the advantages are many. Even if a visit is refused, the person you spoke to hangs up the phone thinking 'that person is keen, they wanted to come and have a look just to prepare for their interview.' Your endeavour and enthusiasm will be noted in a positive light.

The first advantage of a visit is that you will learn some facts to fit into the answers you are constructing. What are the products? Where are the markets? What is the size of the organisation? Does it have a charter or guiding philosophy? If you can work the answers to these questions into your interview, it will be impressive.

Secondly, and perhaps more importantly, you will get a sense of the workplace and its culture. What are the current issues? What are the current problems? What systems are in place? How do people relate to each other? The answer to each of these questions is also valuable information for an interview.

A very important advantage you can gain from a visit is the language of a workplace, including some of the current buzzwords and jargon. When we say that a certain person 'speaks my language' we imply that the person shares some bond of understanding with us. In an interview situation, when the likeability factor is so high, 'speaking the same language' is a major bonus.

Always remember when you make a preliminary workplace visit, that you will also be being judged by the people who are likely to interview you, so conduct yourself accordingly. Have prepared questions ready, do not express too many opinions, and do not outstay your welcome. Fifteen to twenty minutes should give you time to gain the insight and information that you need.

The biggest problem with workplace visits is that on a few occasions the employer has said, 'while you're here we may as well conduct the interview', thus catching the visitor unawares. Be ready to take friendly evasive action if this occurs:

> *'Thank you for the opportunity, but I have people waiting for me at the moment and if I'm not careful I will be late. Anyhow I'm sure to be far more impressive next Tuesday when we're scheduled for the interview.'*

If you feel intimidated by the idea of initiating a workplace visit, or your request for one is refused, at least you should make an incognito visit. Visit as a customer, look in from the street, go to the reception desk and ask for a copy of the annual report. This may give you some feel for the place. At least you will see the type of clothes worn by the people who work there.

However, if you have no direct knowledge of the industry or occupation, you may not want to advertise this fact either at the interview or on a visit. In this case try talking to someone at a different company within the same industry, or to friends or friends of friends who work in the area. Any insight you can gain will prove valuable at the interview.

I recently encouraged a storesperson whom I was coaching to make a workplace visit. He was reluctant because he felt uncomfortable bringing attention to himself; he felt that it would be like enduring the interview twice, once voluntarily! In the end he went along and was surprised that he was made quite welcome. He ended up staying for about half an hour, including a tea break. During this time he discovered that the organisation had recently changed its computer management system because of the limitations of the previous system.

This information was manna from heaven for someone about to be interviewed. He investigated both systems before his interview and so was able to talk about their pros and cons at the interview, making sure that he came to the same conclusion as the organisation had. Luckily the interviewers were not the people he had talked to on his visit, so he was not thought to be merely parroting the information he had been given.

Asking Yourself Question

Once you have some idea of the selection criteria, the likely question areas and, if possible, some of the language used in the workplace, the next step is to ask yourself some possible questions, and prepare answers. You should write these down so they can be edited and revised until you are happy with them. Then you should learn your material, if not off by heart, at least in some detail.

Be warned though, not to sound at the interview as if you are giving an answer learned by rote. Don't over-rehearse; there is such a thing as being too smooth.

The questions that you pose to yourself at this stage should be in their broadest form. If you are going for an interview as a manager or a supervisor then an example might be, 'What are the skills of a manager?' This is a very broad question and it would take some time to answer at an interview, but having thought about it will allow you to select relevant parts and details to suit any more specific question you may be asked. You can also modify this answer if the question is 'What do you see as the primary responsibilities of a manager?' or 'What do you believe a manager's response should be in the following situation?'

Preparing The Answers

The following are a few hints to help in preparing answers to questions. In general, you should prepare the answer in full, from the opening remarks to the closing comments. Too many people study for interviews by merely making a list of the main points they wish to cover. When trying to answer a question at the interview they are not sure how to link the points together, and the answer comes out as a jumbled mess. The best answers are those which have an identifiable structure: a beginning, a middle and an end.

Answer in the First Person

The most powerful language at an interview is in the first person: 'What I have done in the past', 'What I do' and 'What I would do'. Answer in the first person as much as possible.

Many interviewees are uncomfortable using the first person for two reasons: they do not like putting themselves on display by using 'I'; and they fear that continual use of the first person may appear conceited. The reality is that as an interviewee you are on display, like it or not, and not using the first person will not change that.

Many people are so afraid of being seen as conceited at an interview that they avoid speaking in the first person altogether. Of course, speaking in the first person continually—'I can do this, I did that'—can appear conceited, but often this is more a matter of your style than just using the word 'I'. Remember that although appearing conceited does not help your chances at an interview, neither does being too humble.

The most common way of avoiding the first person is to use 'we': 'What we did', 'What we usually do', 'What we would have done'. Some people use the term 'we' excessively at interviews, mainly as a protective mechanism. They feel that they can hide behind 'we' and not put themselves on display, so they cannot be criticised personally for any actions they describe. Look over your shoulder the next time you are at an interview: there is no one else there. The interviewer is interested in you as an individual and this is what must be put on display.

The use of the word 'we' on a few occasions throughout the interview is fine, as it may well be used to demonstrate teamwork, but after each 'we' it is advisable to come back to the first person to explain what your part of the 'we' was. For example, 'We did payroll for eight hundred staff in four days' is fine, providing that you go on to say, 'my part of that work was to input any overtime, allowances ...' and whatever your part of that work was. If at various times you did all parts of the work then this should be made clear: 'We did payroll for eight hundred staff in three days, and at various times I was responsible for each component of the payroll—the tax, the allowances, the deductions ...'

Far worse than the use of 'we' is the use of 'you'. People sometimes think that because they don't like putting themselves on display they will put the interviewers on display instead. It is a lot easier to talk about 'you' than 'me'. This logic will result in phrases such as 'What you could do in that situation is ...'. In one interview I attended a young man was answering in this way and the employer interrupted and said, 'Excuse me, I am not asking you what *I* could do, I am asking you what *you* would do.' This may have been a bit brutal but the employer was essentially asking the applicant to take responsibility for his answer.

Similarly, some interviewees persist in answering 'What *one* could do in this situation ...'. 'We', 'you' and 'one' are all used as buffers to protect the interviewee, and none of these terms is as impressive as 'I'.

Sometimes when people are coached to start using the first person for most of their answers, they start to use other buffers to protect themselves. The two most common of these are: 'I might' and 'I guess'. The thinking behind this is that if you never actually said you would do it, only that if you might, there is a back door that you can escape through. Wrong: there is no back door. The use of 'I might' and 'I guess' gives a bad impression. At one interview when a young man kept prefacing his answers with 'I guess I could do this' and 'I guess I could do that', the employer said:

> 'Let me get this straight. I just want to be sure of what you are saying here. You have no idea what to do in this situation, and you would guess your way out of it. Is that what you are saying?'

The young man tried to explain that he was only using 'I guess' as a figure of speech, but by this stage he had dug a deep and unnecessary hole for himself.

Make Comment

If you meet someone for the first time and you want that person to like you, then you have to give them the opportunity to get to know you. At an interview, you want the interviewer to like you, so you must give them the opportunity to get to know you. Sometimes you will be asked outright to 'tell me about yourself'. An answer should certainly be prepared for this possibility and I discuss this in more detail later, but even such a question doesn't give you the chance to talk about yourself in relation to every facet of the job.

The interview process will usually offer little opportunity to express your inner feelings and beliefs about the various aspects of the job. You must create the opportunity. The easiest way of doing this is to make a comment at the start and end of each major question. These comments, while related to the question at hand, give you the chance to express something about yourself that may not be possible in any other part of the interview. The comments would express your opinion, but can be a chance to express a sense of humour, a pearl of wisdom or an insight into you the person, as opposed to you the worker.

Interviews usually include one or two 'what if' questions, particularly interviews for managerial, supervisory, technical and professional positions. The best way to approach these questions is covered on page 130, but here let's consider how to get the most out of the question by making a comment at the start and at the end of the answer.

> *'Let's say you got the job as a supervisor and one of your staff resents your getting the job and becomes disruptive and tries to undermine your authority. How would you handle this?'*

This question is typical of the type that gets asked at many interviews for supervisory positions, and it lends itself well to a range of preliminary comments. If you are getting on well with the interviewers but you feel that your enthusiasm may be coming across as a little too intense you might try humour:

> *'Would you think the worse of me if I used poison? Running them over in the car park?'*

If you are trying humour, keep a straight face until you've finished and then smile, leaving the interviewers in no doubt that you are joking, and then immediately move on to answer the question in a serious manner. The example given is fairly safe, but all humour runs some risk.

Because of this risk many people are wary of displaying a sense of humour at an interview, but it is an attractive quality in people and therefore can be used to advantage. The idea when using humour is to stay on safe ground and use only predictable, conservative humour. Wait until you get the job before you unleash your wacky self. Sexism and racism have no place at an interview, or anywhere else for that matter. I have seen examples of people effectively disqualifying themselves from consideration for a job by making a smutty sexist joke. If the only humour you know involves a hundred-and-one *double entendres* on the word 'it' then it would be better to get by without any humour at all.

Interviewing a number of people in one day can be a dry, tiring business, and interviewers often appreciate an applicant's attempt to lighten up the interview, even if you are not the world's best humourist.

Overdoing a sense of humour is, of course, worse than no humour at all. As a rule you should introduce humour only once in each forty-minute interview, and certainly no more than twice, or you run the risk of seeming frivolous. It is only possible to use humour three times or more if you are being interviewed for a position as a writer at a greeting card company.

If you decide not to use humour, other opening comments to the question about staff resentment might be:

'I would be disappointed if this happened, but the reality is that it can happen in life, and I feel that knowing how to deal with it, and getting back to business as usual as soon as possible, is part of being a manager.'

'Actually this has happened to me once, and while it wasn't pleasant I found that once people got to know me and my style and the professionalism I bring to my work, then it quickly disappeared.'

'Can I say right at the start that I would see this issue as serious, not because of damage to my own ego, but because undermining any supervisor is undermining the structures we work with and is detrimental to creating a team environment, which I believe is vital to productive, quality work.'

The value of these comments is self-evident; they are making points about your experience, your beliefs, and your ability to integrate into a workplace quickly. Remember that after creating a good image by your comment at the start you still have to go on and answer the question as it was put.

The other advantage of such comments is that they are a subtle way of flattering the interviewers. What you are saying in effect is 'this is a good, relevant, true-to-life question and is worthy of comment.' With the other questions you might play the flattery game a little more directly. For instance, if the question is obviously a difficult one, you can say so out loud: 'That's a difficult question.' If the question contains a few traps then showing you're aware of them is an option, for example saying, 'This question is not as easy as it first appears.'

Interviewers have to sit and try to think of good, testing, relevant questions and receive little direct feedback about their success in achieving this. If you are an interviewer and you work out a question that has hidden difficulties, to hear someone say 'This question is not as easy as it first appears' is recognition of the work that you put into the question and is quite pleasing.

The other place to make a comment is at the end of an answer, thus making full use of the 'primacy' and 'recency' factors which I will explore in the next chapter. Comments at the end of answers can be used in just the same way as starting comments. I will give further examples of how to make opening and closing comments in the section on 'Questions and Answers' on page 109.

Speak from Experience

Speak from experience at every opportunity, particularly in terms of what you have learned from that experience. The start of an answer is a good place to do this. Many interviewees only speak of their experience when directly questioned about their background, but evidence of your experience should appear throughout the interview, not just as the answer to one question.

Prefacing answers with such phrases as, 'A situation similar to this has happened to me and what I learned from the experience was ...' and 'What I have found from my experience is ...' is powerful at an interview. Speaking from experience in this way has two benefits: it shows that you do have experience and that you are not just imagining possibilities; and it indicates that you are the sort of person who can learn the lessons that experience offers.

Don't fall into the trap of thinking that the only experience that counts is direct on-the-job experience. All experience counts, particularly in terms of what you have learned. What does it matter where you gained the experience that taught you a valuable lesson? Often interviewees will omit or undervalue anything that does not relate directly to the job that they are being interviewed for.

Another way of undervaluing your experience is to say things like, 'I *only* have experience in a voluntary capacity', or 'while I don't have any *direct* experience ...'. Leave it to the interviewer to decide how relevant the experience is. Your job is to present your experience, whatever it may be, as lessons learned. Also you should never underestimate the value of the lessons that you have learned just by being alive. If during an interview you say, 'my experience with people in this situation has taught me ...' or 'I have learned from experience that anger is usually not the best response in this situation', and the employer finds these lessons relevant, what does it matter where they were learned?

Passion or Intensity

Another good use of comments is to introduce some of the like-ability factors mentioned earlier, in particular interests and strong feelings. We like people who have special interests and who are intense about some things. Making opening comments such as, 'this is a particular interest of mine' or 'I feel strongly about this area' is an easy way for us to show to the interviewers these qualities.

Make sure, however, that your stated interests are relevant to the position or the qualities needed for the position that you are being interviewed for. As a rule, quality in all its forms—quality of product, quality of delivery, quality of service—is appreciated, while customer service is something you can be intense about. Teamwork might be an area of interest, while the areas of honesty, punctuality, etc., will be important to you.

Many of us are uncomfortable with using the term 'passionate' as one of our personal attributes, but I would suggest you show intensity at least once or twice in an interview. You might say, 'This is an issue close to my heart.' or 'This is an issue that is very important to me.'

If you are going to suggest more than one area of special interest or intensity, make sure the second area is introduced as 'another' area of interest or 'another' passion. This is to let the interviewers know that you are aware of how many times you are using the phrase, and that you are not using it lightly. You don't want to appear as someone who is passionate about everything. If you have more than two passions or particular areas of interest, this will water down the effect. You must decide which facets of the job you are 'passionate' about quite coldly and calculatingly during your preparation.

Analysing Features and Benefits

If you accept that interviews are about selling yourself, then it is worth spending a little time considering how professional sales people are trained. I once had to teach a popular commercial sales skills course, which stressed some of the following points:

Salespeople are taught to think and talk to customers in terms of 'benefits', while the rest of us tend to think in terms of 'features'. Let's take a motor car as an example. It has a whole range of features, some of which may be:

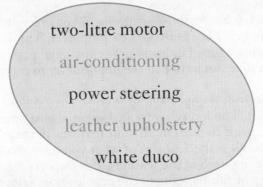

two-litre motor

air-conditioning

power steering

leather upholstery

white duco

Salespeople present each of these features as a benefit to the buyer. The two-litre motor may be presented as being powerful yet good on fuel. The air-conditioning would be for comfort, particularly on those hot, sticky summer days. Each feature would have a corresponding benefit to the buyer. Even the white duco may be presented in this way.

> *'Another good thing about this car is that it is white, which has benefits to you in that it is more easily seen during those danger periods at dusk or dawn, and it reflects the heat so much more in summer and so it is not as hot to get into.'*

Real estate managers make it compulsory for sales staff to be able to name five benefits of each property that they have for sale; not five features, five benefits.

We can and should transfer this sales technique to the interview situation. Most people at an interview talk about the features of what they have to offer, such as:

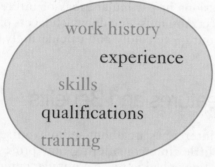

work history

experience

skills

qualifications

training

You need to turn these features into benefits. What is the benefit of your work history to the prospective employer? If you have been in your last position for a long time, the benefit may be that you are reliable and that the new organisation can invest in training you with the confidence that you will stay around and repay that investment.

If you have had various positions in your recent work history, that too can be a benefit to the new employer. This benefit may be that you bring a broad industry or occupational perspective to your new job or that you have had the opportunity to compare different systems.

Your mind-set is important; see yourself as a product that you are trying to sell. The interviewers are potential customers. You have a duty to yourself to present all your features in their best light, as benefits. Review the features of what you have to offer and then list benefits for each of the features. It is important at an interview to be aware of the benefits to the employer of selecting you, and you should include them in the answers you work on in your preparation.

Summary

In summary, this chapter has advised you to:

✔ check for selection criteria

✔ make a workplace visit

✔ write out likely questions and answers

✔ make comments

✔ use the first person

✔ speak from experience at every opportunity

✔ state interest and passion

✔ speak in terms of benefits

If you follow this advice when constructing your answers, during preparation and at the interview, you will be presenting yourself in the best possible light.

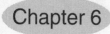

Chapter 6

MAKING THEM REMEMBER YOU

The interview should be a learning process not only for you, but for the interviewers. They should learn about you in both a personal and professional sense, and perhaps also learn something new about the job for which they are interviewing. Of course you will want them to remember you and the points that you made at the interview. How do you make sure that this happens? There are three main principles to remember.

1. Primacy and Recency

The principle of primacy and recency means that people remember the first and last events better than those in the middle. When you attend any information session, you will tend to remember most clearly information given at the start and the end of the session. The longer the session, the more its middle section will become a blur when you think back on it later. This presents some important lessons for interviews.

If you have a choice, try to be the first, or close to the first person interviewed. If this isn't possible, try to be the last or close to the last. These positions give you a small advantage, and although people are able to win jobs from any position on the interview roster, every advantage helps.

The benefit of going first is that if you do well, you become the benchmark for everyone who follows, especially if there are a large number of people being interviewed. It's good for you if your name is mentioned or thought of after each interview as the interviewers consider whether the applicant was as impressive as you.

A colleague of mine was once one of forty applicants interviewed for eight vacant positions. She was the third to be interviewed. She got one of the positions, and found out later that from the fifteenth interview onwards the panel had started taking a photograph of each applicant. This photograph was used to remind the panel who was who when they were discussing the relative merits of each applicant. They decided to take photographs because they were becoming unable to distinguish between the applicants in their memories.

The benefit of being at the end of the interview roster is that their impression of you will have less time to fade when they are talking over the results of all the interviews at the end of the process. Also, panel members may have been disappointed by the standard of the applicants and may have lowered their expectations and given up hope of finding a 'star'. You may be able to restore those expectations, or at least be judged less critically than the earlier applicants.

The principle of primacy and recency also means that you should make full use of the beginning and end of the interview and the beginning and end of each question. Employment psychologists say that the first three minutes of an interview are the most crucial. Most interviewers have formed an opinion of the person they are interviewing during this period, and the rest of the interview will be spent either confirming or refuting this initial opinion. What takes place in the first three minutes are the assessment of appearance, the rituals of first meeting someone, and the first question. It is vital that you do well in these areas to help create an initial favourable image.

The end of the interview is also important. There is nearly always an opportunity towards the end to add any points that you feel you may have overlooked. There is also a chance to make the point that you really want the job. It is just as important to leave with a favourable impression as it is to commence with one.

The beginning and end of each question are also important. A good start to each question can be created by making an interesting comment, as discussed earlier (on page 53), and then giving the answer an identifiable structure. After including the necessary information, a good answer will end with a further comment to round it off nicely.

The worst possible ending is also the most common: 'That's about it really, I can't think of anything else.' This ending essentially says, 'I ran out of answer. I was going along nicely and then I ran out.' I call it the 'plucking apples' answer, as the interviewee is plucking pieces of information from their mind like someone picking apples from a tree: 'There is this piece of information and there is this piece of information and I can't think of any more pieces of information so that must be the end of my answer.'

If you are covering familiar ground the interviewers may go onto 'automatic pilot' especially if they are doing quite a few interviews. On many occasions after an interview a panel member has said to me, 'Did you get that answer?' and I have replied, 'Hang on, you asked the question and the person answered to you.' 'Yes, I know, but I daydreamed through it.'

This is not necessarily a bad thing. If you were not answering well, you would certainly draw much more attention. Interviewers only go on automatic pilot on 'the safe routes', when the answers which they are hearing are what they expected to hear. The problem with interviewers remaining on automatic pilot as you come to the end of your answer is that you will not get the full value of the 'recency' component. There can be no recognition for a good ending to your answer if you don't have the attention of the interviewers.

Your aim should be to bring the interviewers back from automatic pilot as you get to the end of the answer. There are many ways of doing this, such as saying such things as, 'and in conclusion', 'and finally' or 'and the last point is'.

What you are saying in effect is 'come back to me because I am about to finish my answer.' With any lengthy answer, that is of more than a minute or two in duration, make sure you give a clear signal that you are coming to the end, thus bringing the interviewers back from automatic pilot and getting full value for your good ending. If the end of your answer is 'that's about it really, I can't think of anything else'. Let them sleep on. Do not bring them back for this.

2. Mental Images

An anecdote which enables the interviewer to 'see' a favourable picture of you at work is very powerful. When constructing your answers during interview preparation you should include two or three anecdotes to illustrate points.

This advice comes with a major warning, sirens sounding and red lights flashing: some of the worst interviewees are those who turn every question into the opportunity to tell a story. Often it will be a long, involved story which is not obviously relevant to the question being asked. Interviewers are often relieved to get this type of interviewee out of the room as soon as possible, even going so far as not asking all the planned questions to avoid creating another opportunity for a story. Never forget that anecdotal detail is powerful at an interview as long as it is short, sharp and relevant. Anecdotes that are long or not directly to the point will do more harm than good.

I was coaching Carla, a qualified speech therapist, who was

looking for a permanent position in the education industry working with young children. She had previously had a number of temporary jobs in this area. I asked a question that I thought she might be asked at an interview: 'Could you tell me about an area of success that you have had?' This is quite a common question these days. Her first reply was, word for word: 'I have had particular success with children with "F substitution" problems.'

I asked for more detail.

Carla replied, 'But at least one of the interviewers will be a speech therapist, and they will know what I mean by that.' I replied that it didn't matter if each panel member was a speech therapist; it was not a matter of understanding, but Carla getting full value at the interview from her expertise. Try as I might, I couldn't see a picture of someone having success with 'F substitution' problems. I asked Carla for a short anecdote to illustrate her success. After some deliberation this is the story that she told:

> *'I have had particular success with children with "F substitution" problems which, as you know, is the inability to say the "th" sound and instead pronouncing it as "f".*
>
> *'This was a particular problem for one young boy I was working with, because his name was Heath. He pronounced it "Heaf" and, children being children, the other children at school would make fun of him. This started to upset Heath, so much that one day, much to his parents' disappointment, Heath decided to start referring to himself by his middle name of John. A big step for a seven year old.*
>
> *'Heath had about six sessions with me and during these sessions I taught him that it was OK for him to stick his tongue out, or at least between his teeth, when making the "th" sound. This is the problem that these kids have, they do not realise that the tongue goes between the teeth when making the "th" sound. Heath was able to pick up on this and he made good progress. I knew we had the problem beaten when one morning Heath's mother rang me and said, "I wish you could have seen Heath this morning when I dropped him off at school, he was running around to everyone he saw saying, 'My name's Heath, my name's Heath'."'*

Which of Carla's answers is the more powerful?, the eleven word sentence about 'F' substitution or the story about Heath? Which one gives you a picture of a speech therapist working with children and parents in the education service? Which one will remain in your memory? The story of Heath is only the illustration of the technical point, 'I've had particular success with children with "F" substitution problems', but it is the anecdote, the picture, which is the more powerful.

Make sure you prepare a few short, sharp, relevant anecdotes which draw pictures of you working and achieving. Coming up with such anecdotes in the middle of an interview is too difficult—construct them and learn them as part of your preparation.

By using the story of Heath, I have used an anecdote to draw a picture for you. I hope you agree it was more powerful than simply saying 'use a few short, sharp relevant anecdotes'. When I use the story of Heath in group training sessions, I ask at the end, 'What colour hair does Heath have?' Each time there are people in the group who tell me, because the picture is so powerful that they can 'see' Heath. The story of Heath is a good model to follow because it draws a powerful picture and yet only takes forty seconds to tell.

3. From the Known to the Unknown

When we are children we are constantly learning new things. A lot of the information is so new that we have no memory 'file' to store it in; the information doesn't relate directly to anything else we have learned so far. As children we continually create new files in which to store new information. As we get older, the ability to continually create new files practically stops. There are no vacant files remaining. Thankfully this does not mean that we cannot learn anything new, but it does mean that all new information must go into old files.

This has relevance to the job interview situation. Many interviewees make the mistake of assuming interviewers' knowledge. They see it as patronising to give the interviewers information which they think is common knowledge within the industry or occupation. This mistake is especially common when the position is an internal promotion or when for some other reason the interviewers are known by the job-seeker. They may think, 'The people who are interviewing me know me well and therefore I can assume that they know I have certain experience and knowledge.'

Wrong! Assume nothing. Assume nothing even if the interviewers are people you know and have worked with for some time. If you accept that learning is going on a journey to a new place, then as adults we can't go on that journey unless it starts from a place we know.

It is flawed logic to decide not to tell the interviewers what you think they should already know. After all, the interviewers know the answer to nearly every question they ask. The reason they ask is to give you the chance to show that you also know the answers.

If you didn't tell interviewers what they already should know, most interviews would be over in five minutes, and that wouldn't be to your advantage.

Don't forget that it is your job at an interview to lead the interviewers from the known to something they may not know about you. To do this you must start your answers with information they already know. In effect you are saying, 'this is the memory file that you must open to accept the new information I'm about to give you.'

The easy way to do this and not seem patronising is start with the words, 'as you know'. For example, let's say you have keyboard skills, and you are being interviewed for a job as a secretary. In the last few months you have learned a new word processing package called 'Quickpro', which is by far the best word processing package you have ever used. At the interview you are asked, as word processing operators often are, 'Which do think is the best word processing package?' This gives you a chance to demonstrate your up-to-date knowledge. The worst answer you could give is, 'Quickpro': a one-word answer. This is merely seeing the question as a request for information and supplying that information.

If the interviewers have never heard of 'Quickpro', their attention will be lost while they try to understand this new information. In this case the interviewers will not come on this journey with you to learn about 'Quickpro'. Their body language will indicate this uncertainty as they hastily look at each other: *'Quickpro? What's that? Is that a new package? Has anybody else heard of that package?'*

The better way to answer the question would be to start with what the interviewers know and then move them to the unknown, for example:

> *'As you know there are a number of word processing packages on the market, and the most common of these are probably "Word for Windows" and "Word Perfect". I have used these and they do a reasonable job, they have their strong points and their weaknesses. Recently I've had experience with a new package and I think it is the best so far. Its name is "Quickpro" and it is the best because ...'*

Which file do the interviewers open to put in the new information? The file with 'Word for Windows' and 'Word Perfect' in it. By starting in this way, from a place the interviewers know, they can now learn about 'Quickpro' easily, and with interest.

The learning principle, 'From the Known to the Unknown', teaches us two things:

✔ never assume interviewers' knowledge

✔ always start your answer with information you think the interviewers know before moving on to the unknown.

The three learning principles we have covered in this chapter, Primacy and Recency, Mental Images and From the Known to the Unknown, should always be kept in mind when you are constructing answers during your preparation, and at an interview.

Chapter 7

PRESENTING
THE WORDS

The second part of your preparation should be practising how you are going to present the words that you have composed in the first part of your preparation. This second phase is at least as important as finding the words. When you do a public speaking course, you learn that between seventy and ninety per cent of your message does not come from the words you use, but from body language, eye contact, tone, emphasis, facial expression and gestures. It is a staggering figure—seventy to ninety per cent! If you devote most of your interview preparation time on preparing the words, you are leaving out up to seventy per cent of your message.

Body Language

In day-to-day life, we rely on reading non-verbal communication to gain an insight into other people. Body language is so important that if we notice a clash between what is said and what body language tells us we tend to believe the body language, not the words. This is certainly true in the interview situation.

Try this: sit on the edge of your chair with your legs and body in a straight line and only your shoulders and bottom touching the back of the chair. Now interlock your fingers and rest your hands on your stomach. Say out loud, 'I'm very enthusiastic.'

It feels odd, doesn't it? You can say 'I'm very enthusiastic' all day, but if your body language is saying otherwise, no one will believe you. Sitting like this would definitely give the wrong message if you wanted to convince the interviewers that you were indeed enthusiastic.

The best way to sit at an interview is towards the front of your chair (not at the edge) with your back straight, leaning forward slightly. Your legs should be together, tucked slightly in towards the chair. Your hands in the resting position should be just up from your knees and from there should be used regularly to make appropriate gestures.

This position is seen as displaying enthusiasm, commitment, and desire. If you sat back in the chair with your arms folded, you could use the same words but you would not do nearly as well as the person who sat forward. Of course there may be very enthusiastic people who just happen to like sitting back with their arms folded, but what we are dealing with is other people's perceptions.

It doesn't help good communication to put barriers between you and the interviewers, so do not fold your arms. Men should not cross their legs either. Women's crossed legs are seen as a necessary modesty barrier, and will not inhibit conversation as it can do with men. However, women's legs should be crossed below the knee, rather than above the knee.

The best image that you can create at the start of an interview is one of willing participation, but this is not always how you feel at an interview. When you are nervous, your every instinct is to protect and defend yourself. If we sat as we felt, most of us would have arms and legs folded, thinking, 'I know you have at least one trick question in here somewhere.' This is another reason why it is important to see interviews as a performance, and to play the part. To do this you have to understand how a willing participant is perceived, and to practise this during your preparation.

Never allow your body language to indicate a feeling of superiority. Even if the interviewers are younger and less experienced than you, do not interlock your fingers and put them on top of or behind your head, as this may make the interviewers feel the need to defend their position of power. The last thing you need at an interview is a power game between you and the interviewers.

Voice

The tone of your voice is another factor that can make a difference at an interview. If you speak in a monotone, you will sound boring and you may have trouble keeping the interviewers' attention. You may also give them the feeling that you are a boring person, or that you are disinterested or lifeless. They certainly won't be convinced that you are a motivated go-getter.

We expect people who are interested, interesting and enthusiastic to vary their tone of voice. We also expect them to emphasise areas of interest, speed up or slow down depending on the point being made, and use various facial expressions to support what is being said.

Many people make the mistake of preparing the words to be used at an interview without any idea of how they will be presented. If you believe that in the past you have had a great set of words but the interviewers have not responded as you had hoped, the problem is probably your delivery. But don't despair: delivery can be improved with practice just as content can.

The Pitch

By the 'pitch' of an interview I mean its level of formality or informality. It is not true that interviews have to be very formal and that answers must be presented accordingly.

Of course formal interviews are sometimes unavoidable, but your aim as an interviewee should be to temper the formality as much as you can. Try to make the interview as conversational as possible even though it is generally a one-sided conversation, with you doing most of the talking. You should speak to the interviewers as though you were talking to acquaintances, if not friends, as though you trust them enough to take them into your confidence, while being careful not to be so familiar that you are seen as taking liberties.

In constructing your answers be guided by conversational English. Don't use words or phrases that you are not comfortable with, and above all don't assume false airs and graces. Remember that one of the factors in increasing likeability is honesty (see page 15). It is hard to appear an honest person if an interviewer believes that you are behaving artificially and hiding your true self.

Think of the telephone. Most of us hate talking to someone who is obviously using a 'phone voice'. (Is this where the word 'phoney' came from?) Unfortunately, a large number of people take the 'phone voice' mentality into the interview room. They seem to be trying to be something they are not, and they make both themselves and the interviewers uncomfortable. They do not do well.

If you can achieve a conversational pitch at an interview, the results can be spectacular. One of my clients was at an interview for nearly two hours, not undergoing a long interrogation, but in a friendly, involved conversation. The time passed quickly and pleasantly.

Towards the end of the interview one of the interviewers looked at the clock and said, 'My goodness, has anyone noticed the time?' They bundled my client out as quickly as possible, mainly because someone else had been waiting for their interview. The next day, two of the panel rang her, independently of each other, to continue their conversation. I had a fair idea that she would get the job.

On the other hand, interviews can certainly be too informal. Sometimes the most difficult interviews are conducted by one person who wants to be very informal and have a discussion over a cup of coffee. In many ways this should be the easiest kind of interview, as the likeability factors are likely to be dominant. But you should never let the informality lure you into forgetting that an interview is always a competition, and that more than one person is being interviewed.

A difficult part of this type of interview is accepting the cup of coffee without spilling it or rattling the cup and saucer too much because of nervousness. One man once accepted my offer of a cup of coffee at an interview. He took sugar, but by the time the spoon had reached his cup there were only a few grains of sugar left, and a white trail of sugar across the table. If this might be you, politely decline the coffee, saying that you 'just had one thank you, but I certainly don't mind if you have one'.

Eye Contact

Correct use of eye contact is important but it has to be considered in the context of body language and facial expression. At an interview you should try for the kind of eye contact that is part of a co-operative manner; this eye contact is usually accompanied by an open body stance and the nodding of your head to acknowledge points when someone is speaking to you. Staring and glaring are out.

Some interviewees are so nervous that they seem to be showing intensity rather than creating a look which conveys being earnest and committed to the cause. Other interviewees try deliberately to create an air of intensity believing that intensity is a positive factor at an interview.

Be careful that you are not intentionally or unintentionally appearing too intense. Do not confuse dedication, commitment, enthusiasm or passion with intensity. If you think back to the section on likeability, you'll recall that interesting and passionate people tend to be attractive to others. However, most of us are not attracted to people who are too intense. During the interview a topic may arise on which you have genuine strong feelings. To show intensity on one such occasion is fine, as long as it is tempered by the rest of your interview. If you are a naturally intense person be aware that this can be damaging if shown too strongly at an interview. You may need to do some work on the more co-operative forms of body language and eye contact, and smiling more could be a good start.

Eye contact should begin during the introductions at the start of the interview, and be maintained throughout. To do this you need to keep your head up, which will also help to create the impression that you are confident. The first sign that an interviewee is having trouble with a question, or losing confidence, is usually the loss of eye contact, either through the dropping of the head or, in more serious cases, by shielding the eyes with a hand.

Displaying confidence at an interview is difficult if you are nervous, as it is if you are a shy person or someone who suffers low self-esteem. Remember that you are putting on a performance and you have to appear a confident person for the length of the interview—not to *be* confident, to *appear* confident. Some of the world's foremost actors are shy people at heart.

What happens if your performance at the interview helps you to get the job, but later the interviewers discover that you are not the person they thought you were? This happens in many cases: what happens is that you have gained an opportunity to demonstrate your ability to do the job. Successful interviewees can only get jobs, they cannot keep them. Only performance on the job can do that.

When I first started coaching people in job interview techniques, most interviews were one-to-one. In recent years there has been an increasing trend away from a single interviewer. Even small organisations are starting to use at least two interviewers, and larger organisations are using three or more. This may explain why I usually refer to interviewers, plural.

I believe the trend to more than one interviewer has come about for two reasons. It can indicate the internal politics of an organisation. If there is a lack of trust between competing factions, each will feel the need to be represented on the interview panel so they can keep an eye on each other. Perhaps Personnel and Accounts do not trust each other to select the right person, so at the interview there is someone from both Personnel and Accounts. Secondly, as more laws are introduced to ensure fairness, organisations use more than one interviewer to protect interviewers from charges of prejudice such as sexism, racism, favouritism or nepotism.

Having more than one interviewer doesn't necessarily prevent discrimination, but it does add authority to a decision, and it is hard for someone who believes they have been treated unfairly to charge that collusion and conspiracy took place. More than two interviewers is a waste of energy and resources and usually shows organisational inefficiencies. But whether there are one, two or six interviewers, your basic approach to the interview should not alter.

You do, however, have to think differently about eye contact when there are several interviewers. Usually one person is designated the head of the panel, and that person will be the one to come out and get you and introduce you to the rest of the panel. (This situation is discussed in the 'The Interview' Chapter 9, page 104.) Usually the head of the panel will ask the first question, but whoever asks it should receive the focus of your reply. That is, the most of your eye contact should be with the person who asks the question, and after each major point (in effect, each paragraph of your learned preparatory notes), you should try to catch the eyes of the other panel members to let them know you are also speaking to them. You may see only the tops of heads because some of the interviewers will be taking notes. Don't be disconcerted by this, it is natural that it should happen; just hope to catch each person's eye at least once during each answer.

The second question is usually asked by another member of the panel and then the panel members will alternate in asking questions. The person who asks the second question should now receive your primary focus, and the person who asked the first question should become one of the interviewers with whom you try to have eye contact after each major point has been made.

The worst thing you can do is to continually focus your attention on the head of the panel, regardless of who asks the question. Some interviewees do this because they think that the head of the panel will make the decision, that power attracts like a magnet. This is wrong for two reasons. Firstly, it is rude to the other panel members—you are in effect dismissing them, and they will notice it and dislike you for it. Secondly, the head of the panel will not like it either because interviewing is very tiring work, and the reason questions are shared is to deliberately spread the focus of your attention in order to make the interview less tiring.

This is so important that there is a simple yet powerful game to play which leaves each panel member in no doubt that you consider them important. When a question is being asked by someone new, put your hands on your chair by your sides, and then be seen to lift and move yourself slightly in the direction of the person who is now asking the question. Your body language is clearly stating that you are changing the focus of your attention.

With a small panel it may be possible to simply turn your head a few degrees to address a different panel member, but this is not the same message. Always be seen to lift yourself slightly towards the new person.

Rushing into an answer shows immaturity. Warning bells will start ringing for an interviewer if they ask a question and no sooner are the words out of their mouth than the answer is coming back at them. This is particularly so if the question is considered an important one, requiring some thought. Answers that are rushed into often miss the point, overlook vital information, lack structure or just fade away to nothing at the end.

If you are to avoid rushing into an answer, then there should be a period of silence, a pause, before you reply. Unfortunately, most speakers do not handle silences well in any form of public speaking. Usually speakers fill silences with 'ums' and 'ahs' or the ever present 'you know'. Filling the silences in this way will not help you at an interview.

When asked a major question, a good strategy is to break eye contact and show that you are thinking. Each of us has our own idiosyncrasy which denotes that we are thinking. Mine is to look up and hold the back of my neck with my left hand. I was coaching my brother and when I asked him to do this, he looked silly. His way of showing he is thinking is to look down and hold his nose at the spot between his eyes with the thumb and forefinger of his right hand.

Whatever your way of showing you are thinking, you should employ it each time you are asked a major question. You can repeat the question out loud so the interviewers know you are taking time to think. But you must make sure you break eye contact. When you have your thoughts in order, which could take up to ten seconds, regain eye contact. This is your signal to the interviewers that you are ready to begin your answer.

This technique has a number of advantages. First of all, it creates a gap in which you can put your thoughts in order and consider your answer. Breaking eye contact and repeating the question out loud also avoids the problem of rushing into answers, and so appearing immature. Another bonus of this strategy is that it is a subtle form of flattery. In effect you are saying, 'This is a good question and it deserves a considered answer. What I am doing now is considering my answer. I am a considerate sort of person. I am the sort of person who thinks before they act.' These are all good impressions to make.

You are also giving the interviewers a short rest, which they will appreciate. Some interviewees are painful to behold as they grimace in their struggle to compose an answer. In addition by breaking eye contact and showing you are thinking, you are demonstrating to the interviewers you are not going to display an awkward struggle to reply.

All good strategies can be spoiled if they are overdone, and this one is no exception. Make sure you only employ it for the major questions, as employing it all the time can create a negative reaction. Another example of when not to employ this strategy is if you are asked a question such as, 'Why did you apply for this job?' Try this: pretend you are at an interview, assume your normal thinking position and then say out loud, 'Why did I apply for this job?' Feels silly, doesn't it? You should know why you applied for a job without having to stop and think.

You should use the pausing strategy for each of the major questions, even if the question is one which you have second-guessed and consequently could answer immediately. Outwardly you may be looking up and rubbing the back of your neck with one hand while saying out loud, 'How would I do that?', but inwardly you may be thinking, 'Great! Just the question I hoped they would ask.'

Gestures

When under any form of public scrutiny one of two things usually happens to our gestures: we under-react or we over-react. Either our natural gestures disappear altogether, or we become hyperactive and overdo the gestures. At an interview a lack of gestures may suggest that you are uncomfortable in the presence of the interviewers, while too many gestures may be distracting. I have seen people who are naturally in the habit of making gestures lock their hands together between their knees in the belief that using gestures is not good at interviews.

The secret is to appear natural. If you are the sort of person who naturally makes gestures, continue to do so. If you are the sort of person who does not make gestures at all, then you will have to learn at least a few. I did not say to *be* natural, I said to *appear* natural. We take the natural use of gestures as a signal that someone is comfortable in our presence, which is exactly what you should be trying to achieve. Practise at least a few gestures until they look natural.

The important gestures are those that support your words. If you are saying that something concerns you, it is vital to look concerned at the same time or it will be difficult for the interviewer to believe you. Remember the exercise on enthusiasm.

I was coaching a supervisor who was being interviewed for a manager's position. She told me she had successfully supervised the integration of two different sections of her office. This ranked high on her achievements and was a good point to make. I suggested that when making this point at the interview she should hold her hands out in front of her chest and slowly join them. I wanted to *see* a successful merger as well as hear of one. This example illustrates how much effort you should put into your preparing your presentation. It can make the difference between a good interview and a great interview.

Summary

In this chapter on presenting the words we have considered the importance of:

✔ non-verbal communication

✔ the pitch of the interview

✔ voice

✔ eye contact

✔ pausing before answering

✔ gestures

These factors, together with the material covered in the chapters 'Finding the Words' and 'Making Them Remember You' will show you where to put your efforts in preparing for an interview.

By now you must realise that successful interviews do not just happen, but are the result of hard work. Many people are not prepared to do this work, which may explain why the standard of performance at most interviews is not high.

You must also realise that much of the preparation assumes that you will be able to work out the interview questions ahead of time. To some extent this is true. Of course it is not possible to anticipate every question, but in doing the preparation you are highly likely to second-guess some questions and prepare some good answers. The knowledge of how to structure answers to any question which may arise also makes it much easier to deal with unexpected questions. In the coming chapters I will look at questions of structure.

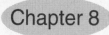

Chapter 8

WHAT DO THEY LOOK FOR?

In the chapter 'How the Interviewer Sees It' I listed the selection factors that most employers take into consideration when choosing someone to fill a vacant position. We will now consider some of these factors in more detail to see how you can persuade interviewers that you meet the needs of each selection factor. In addition we will look at a few extra factors not always thought of as being influential at interviews.

I will illustrate the selection factors with some hypothetical interview questions and answers. It is important to know that I do not recommend that you learn these suggested answers off by heart. This is because although the structure and content will be accurate, the words are mine, and it is important that the words in your answers are yours. It is hard to appear honest and natural at an interview if you are using someone else's words.

Sometimes the answers I give will not be grammatically correct. This is because I am reporting answers which I have actually heard at interviews, and most of us speak differently to how we write. Interviews are about the spoken rather than the written word and I am trying to capture this in the answers.

Skills

It amazes me how many people will not recognise their own skills unless they have some sort of diploma or certificate to prove them. Many of life's skills are not taught in universities or colleges. When was the last time you saw a diploma of problem solving, a certificate for working well under pressure, or a degree in giving priority order to four competing pieces of work?

You may be fortunate enough to have a document which officially recognises a particular skill, and it does make it easier to promote this skill at an interview. However, having a certificate to say you have learned a skill and being able to demonstrate that you can use it to the employer's benefit are two completely different things. Of the two, being able to demonstrate that you can use the skill is by far the most powerful at an interview.

We are in the age of transferable skills, which means simply that employers are now, more than at any other time in history, prepared to accept that what is learned at one workplace is relevant at another workplace. Most employers will acknowledge that skills can transfer from one job to another, one industry to another and one occupation to another. However, you may still meet the occasional dinosaur among employers who has to be convinced of this.

Any skills learned in your cumulative life experience may be worth raising at an interview including skills learned outside the workplace, at schools, colleges or on short courses, skills learned in hobbies, through participation in clubs or in volunteer work. All are relevant as long as you are able to demonstrate at the interview that you can use the skill to the benefit of the employer. To do this you have to be able not only to state that you have a skill, but indicate what that skill will enable you to do and how you would use it in your work. Too often applicants believe it is enough to list their skills or display supporting documents, without finding the words to demonstrate their value to the employer. This is the difference between merely presenting information and selling yourself for the job.

Naturally, you can't promote the benefits of your skills at an interview if you do not recognise them yourself. Make a list of all your skills, regardless of how minor you think they may be. Sometimes in doing this it is difficult to differentiate between skills and personal qualities, so instead of attempting to separate them, list them all. Is the ability to deal with angry clients a skill or a personal quality? Who knows? Who cares? Put it on the list.

Once you have your list, work out which of the skills may be useful to demonstrate at an interview, according to the job applied for. As you apply for different jobs the skills you may need to demonstrate will vary. Once you have decided you have a skill and can demonstrate how you would use it, be proud of it; do not apologise for it. The fact that you may have initially learned the skill in a voluntary or non-workplace capacity or have not used the skill for some time is irrelevant to its value now.

Let's see how to get full value out of your skills at an interview. In this example, an applicant for a draftsperson's job is asked about their ability to use computers. The interviewer wants to find out whether the job-seeker is familiar with computer drafting and design packages. Most people in the drafting profession are familiar with at least one package. However, in this example the interviewee is also able to use spreadsheets, word processors and do some basic programming.

> *'Computers are becoming an essential tool in more and more fields. Drafting is no exception. Can you tell us what computer experience you have had, and what you feel the value of computers in the drafting field to be?'*

This is a major question. Most likely it relates directly to a key selection criterion which requires, 'the ability to use computer drafting and design packages'. If this were the case then the question should be no surprise to any applicant and should have been covered in their preparation. I would hope that the interviewee had some form of this question written down and had brought it to the interview with an answer in note form.

Here is a poor answer:

> *'I have had extensive experience in using computer drafting and design packages and I believe that they are the way to go, they just make work so much easier.'*

A better answer would be:

> *'I have had a deal of experience in computer drafting and design over a period of four years. I am able to use all the most common packages although I prefer and have had most experience on Prodraft. I can use every facet of the program right through to completed and fully detailed drawings.*
>
> *'You mentioned that computers are becoming essential and I agree. I can't imagine being without one now. I enjoy working on the computer so much so that I have also learned to do word processing, spreadsheets and basic programming.'*

Although better, this answer still doesn't get full value for the job-seeker's skills, particularly word processing, spreadsheet and basic programming. This answer also neglects to include any comment at the start or the end of the answer, gives little insight into the interviewee, and is barely conversational.

Here is a really good answer:

> *'Certainly it was your emphasis on computer use which attracted me to apply for this job in the first place. It is my belief that the advent of computer drafting and design packages is the most exciting change to take place in our industry—probably ever. I have been using computers in my work since the first*

packages became available. I actually put myself through a night school course over six years ago. The second and third generation packages are certainly a great improvement on the first packages even though it is only six years down the track.

'You mentioned, when asking the question, that computers are becoming essential and I agree. They are making our work easier and, I believe, more interesting. Organisations and individuals that do not embrace the new technology will become dinosaurs and die away. Computer drawing has two main benefits that can and should be utilised: it is quicker on the more complicated jobs, and they are more accurate. Having said this there are still some simple jobs that, by the time I have turned the computer on and got into the package, I could have finished by hand, and the accuracy still depends on the information that is fed into the machine.

'One of the benefits of this speed on the more complicated jobs is that it encourages innovation, which in the end gives us a better product. It's a lot easier if you have a drawing on a computer screen to say, "What would it look like if we changed this section?" and just have a look at it. Without the computer, to draw up a whole new plan to see the effects of one small change was inhibiting.

'The benefits to us also transfer into benefits for our customers, which helps us to stay competitive. I see more and more that the customers are expecting to see computers in use. For instance, they are asking to see a range of detailed options; the incorporation of some of their own ideas. This work is a lot easier on computer.

'Of course to get these benefits it is necessary to have the computer skills. I have the skills and I am happy to demonstrate them for you, and please ask my referees about my skills in this area. I also have word processing skills and I like to do my own reports. I find that by the time that I have given a report to office support to type for me, got it back, checked it, and had it altered it is more efficient to do it myself. This also has the benefit of saving on office support costs.

'I am also able to do spreadsheets and some basic programming. The benefit of these skills is that I can use them to quickly set up a system to do any repetitive calculations that a project may need, again saving time and money. If there are skills and systems here that I do not know then I am happy to learn them, if I have skills that other people need I am happy to pass them on.

'In conclusion I would like to say that computers are a tool and like any tool their use should be considered when there are benefits to be gained. Computers are not magic and will never

replace the need to be diligent or innovative in problem solving,
and computers will never ever have the personal skills that are
necessary when dealing with customers.'

Experience

The value of speaking from experience at every opportunity has
been emphasised in the chapter 'Finding the Words'. The rules are
the same as those just described for examining and promoting your
skills. Remember, all the experience in the world is useless unless
you can demonstrate what the experience taught you and how you
would use it.

Let's look at an example in my own area of skills and experience,
running training courses. At an interview I am asked, 'Do you have
any experience in running training courses for young people?'

First of all, what is a bad answer to this question?

If I do have this experience the worst answer I could give is say
only, 'Yes, I do'. This response goes nowhere near giving me full
benefit for the experience that I have.

A better, but still not good, answer would be:

> *'Yes I have run several training courses for young people. My*
> *position at Acme Corp involved running personal development*
> *courses for all the company apprentices, and I did this for the*
> *first two years I was at Acme Corp. Later I moved on to super-*
> *visor, then finally management training.'*

Clearly this is better than simply saying 'Yes, I do', but it still falls
into the trap of only providing the information asked for, with a
little indication of broader experience gained and the progression
from training trainees to training management. The answer does
nothing to reveal the lessons that I have learned in training young
people: remember, it is not the experience itself but the lessons
learned from it that is important at interview. I can't say too many
times, experience means little, lessons everything.

An even better answer would be:

> *'Yes I have and I quite enjoyed it really, although it proved to*
> *be quite a challenge at first. The first two years I was at Acme*
> *Corp I ran the personal development training for all the com-*
> *pany apprentices.*
>
> *'I quickly learned that training young people was not the*
> *same as training older people. I think it's because they had just*
> *come out of school and were expecting to be treated more like*
> *children than adults. I found that I had to work harder at*
> *breaking the ice and on the introductions at the start of training*

*in order to get them to open up more and talk about themselves
and their opinions.*

*'I found that young people were also far more responsive to
active learning and so I incorporated more games and role
plays to keep their attention up. Later when I moved on to
supervisor training and eventually management training I
found that I missed the apprentices and so I managed to
arrange the occasional session back with them.*

*'Training people of different age groups is easier if they are
in groups consisting wholly of their own age. It is harder if you
have groups which have a mixture of younger and older people.
In this case, finding the right balance and giving everybody
access to air their views can sometimes be hard work.'*

This is a longer answer but it is not a long answer. It is structured
well and is concise about the points that it makes. If this answer
had been much longer it might have needed a summary at the end
or an 'in conclusion' to bring the interviewers back from automatic
pilot.

This answer follows the rules. It is in the first person. It starts
with a comment. In this case the comment reveals that not only do
I have experience in training young people but that I enjoyed it,
and it also adds a touch of humility and honesty to my interview to
say, 'I found it to be quite a challenge at first.' The answer gives the
information requested about the experience but it also illustrates
the lessons learned from the experience. It brings in a progression
of experiences in a logical way, and it finishes with a comment. It is
conversational. It demonstrates more personality than the first two
responses, and therefore more likeability. On the whole it is a much
better answer.

In this I had the advantage of being able to refer to the experience of training apprentices. That is, if you accept that I did not
make it up completely (I do not advocate telling lies). But what if I
did not have the experience?

If I knew what was needed to work with young people without
having had the experience, that is, if I knew about the need for
more time and the need for more emphasis on active learning, then
I would an experience to show this if I possibly could. Suppose I
had trained five young people among thousands of older people in
my first two years at Acme Corp,I would present the information in
this way:

*'Yes I have and I quite enjoyed it really, although it proved to
be quite a challenge at first. The first two years I was at Acme
Corp I trained a number of young people, and I quickly
learned that it was not the same as training the older people.'*

Is this telling a lie? I don't believe so. How many is a number? Five is a number, isn't it? This is just presenting the information in the best possible light. If the lessons that I refer to are correct, the actual number of young people that I trained is unlikely to be an issue. If I could not find any experience, no matter how hard I looked, I would begin:

> *'I am looking forward to training young people. I know it is not the same as training older people. In the first instance many of them are just out of school and ...'*

This is clearly avoiding the question as it was asked, but I would try to convey my understanding of working with young people before I was stopped. If I was able to get away with this I would finish by saying:

> *'So while I have not yet had the opportunity to work with young people I do have an understanding of what it takes and I am looking forward to working in that area.'*

It is better to approach the answer in this way than to begin, 'I do not have any experience in training young people although I do have an understanding of what is required.' The better way gives the panel the opportunity to write me up (or in a less formal process, think of me) in the following way:

> *Selection criterion 4: The ability to run training courses for young people:*
> *'While Philip did not have any direct experience in this area he was able to demonstrate a good understanding of the skills and knowledge needed to be successful.'*

Try to remove any negative elements from your answers, if not completely, then for as long as possible, at least until after you have indicated some positives.

Qualifications

There are some jobs where the qualifications are mandatory and that is that. Imagine someone getting a job as a doctor without a degree in medicine. Some people try, but if they succeed and we catch them, we lock them up.

However, there are many other jobs where qualifications are stated as mandatory, but in fact they are not. As with length of experience, qualifications are often unnecessarily stated as essential to cut down the number of applicants to manageable numbers.

Newspaper employment ads may ask for qualifications so that

any customers of the company who may read the advertisement can see that it only employs qualified staff. In fact, experienced people without qualifications are often accepted. This practice is very common in trades areas such as dealerships. A newspaper advertisement may require 'qualified motor mechanics', but a check on the company's staff would reveal people working as mechanics who had learned on the job and had no formal qualifications. Don't let lack of qualifications stop you from applying for positions unless you are sure that the qualifications specified are really mandatory.

If you feel lack of qualifications is denying you interview opportunities even if you are looking for work in an area where qualifications are not mandatory, try enrolling in a course. As soon as the course starts, add 'part-way through' whatever course it is to your résumé and application. This technique has opened doors for some of my clients. If you get the job it is up to you whether or not you go on to finish the course, while you are working.

If you actually have qualifications, remember that other applicants also may have them, and a decision will depend on who can best demonstrate that they can use the qualifications to advantage. If you do have qualifications, be proud of them! It is not helpful when graduates say they '*only*' have a Bachelor of Arts', instead of selling the research and writing skills necessary to gain such a degree.

If you have a certificate, or other record of qualification, take it along and show it at the interview. If you have a number of qualifications, take the most relevant ones; don't take them all unless you are going for a base-grade or entry-level position. In that case take them all along, as they may be just that extra push you need to be selected.

Achievements

One of the easiest ways to demonstrate the value of your skills, knowledge, qualifications and experience is to talk about your achievements. Achievements can be very powerful at an interview if presented correctly. And yet, it is surprising how many confident, competent people cannot recall any achievements worthy of note when asked.

Make sure that you don't fall into this trap. List your achievements, and learn them as part of your preparation. One of the reasons many people can't recall their achievements is the belief that unless the achievements are earth shattering they are not worth talking about.

We are living in an age of self-aggrandisement, with untold numbers of self-proclaimed successful entrepreneurs and business leaders giving lectures on their achievements: 'I liked the product so much I bought the company.' This attitude is supported by a media which persists in lionising certain people and making them into heroes. Therefore it is not surprising that ordinary people feel that their smaller achievements are not valuable. I coached one man who had been paid a minimum of $250 000 per year for each of his last three jobs. When I raised the issue of achievements he said, 'Sorry Philip, off the top of my head I can't think of any achievements.' What nonsense!

Organisations become successful because of the cumulative effect of the staff's many small achievements. If you revised a work system and made it more efficient, that is an achievement, regardless of it being a filing system or a system for accepting million-dollar tenders. If some action of yours won back a disaffected client, that is an achievement, and so is learning new skills while still maintaining your work outputs.

Interviewers have their failings, but one positive thing in their favour is that they do tend to acknowledge the small achievements that interviewees describe. Make sure that they hear about your achievements.

In raising your accomplishments at the interview make sure you get full value for them. To do this you must link your wisdom to the achievement. It is not enough to say, 'One achievement that I am proud of is that I won back one of Acme Corp's major clients who had become disaffected and given his business to our competitor. This resulted in a one million dollar contract being returned to Acme Corp.'

This is a fantastic achievement, and certainly one to be presented at interview. However, presented in the form shown it is grossly undersold because it demonstrates no wisdom.

A better way would be:

> *'One of the achievements that I am proud of during my time at Acme Corp was winning back a major client who had become disaffected and given his business to our major competitor. The business was worth a million dollars a year to Acme Corp so this was no small thing. When we first heard of the loss it came as quite a blow and there were people running around wringing their hands together saying "we'll have to put off staff" and the like.*
>
> *'My experience in these matters told me that worrying would not help and that the only thing that would help was winning the business back or winning replacement business. I contacted the client to find out why the business had been taken away. At*

first they were not inclined to speak to me, but I persisted and found it to be a range of reasons which would fall under the general umbrella of complacency, particularly in the area of sales and delivery—neither of which were areas under my control, it was a relief to find out. One of the main points was that the client had discovered that we had been selling to one of his competitors at a cheaper rate on no greater volume.

'The end result was that I drew up a service contract which broadened our original agreement to include guarantees on delivery and price, as well as quality. After an apology from us about previous problems and some lengthy negotiations, we were able to bring the client back into the fold, and to the best of my knowledge the client remains there still. The other thing I instigated was a review of standards to make sure that we did not have similar problems with other clients who may also have been about to leave. What could have been a disaster turned into a positive if painful learning experience about maintaining standards of service.'

This is a better answer because it links the lessons learned through experience to the achievements. Not all of us have won back a million-dollar client. But whatever our achievements we do need to present them in the best possible light.

The majority of interviewees, if they think to mention their achievements at all, dwell exclusively in the past, on what they have already achieved, without looking ahead to what they may still achieve. It is imperative that you also have a sound idea of what you may achieve over time in the job you are applying for. If you get it, how will you judge your own success over time? You may be asked this question directly but even if you are not, you should include it in your interview. For example, let's say that you are being interviewed for a job as area sales representative. At some stage in the interview it would be a good idea to say something like this:

'I would be disappointed if over the first few months I could not demonstrate to all current customers that they would receive at least the same standard of service that they are receiving now, while at the same time increasing the client base and increasing the value of the average order from all clients.'

This is clearly setting out what you would want to achieve if you were successful in the position. This answer is especially appropriate if you know that the previous incumbent was well thought of. If you knew the former employee had been sacked for being lazy then achieving the same standard would hardly be impressive.

Instead you would have to explain your strategy for improving the standard of service.

Ability to Communicate

What a double-edged sword the 'ability to communicate' is! The applicant has to demonstrate their past ability to communicate while presently communicating directly to the potential employer. Which is more important, the past or the present?

The answer is the present. How you communicate at the interview will create the primary evaluation of your communication skills, and no amount of bumbling about how well you have got on with, negotiated against, spoken or written to, other people at other times will overcome this assessment. Even if you do communicate well at the interview, remember to demonstrate your skills further by using examples of previous communication ability. Also, don't forget that in many jobs, communication skills include written communication. In this case take along a good example of your written work: in this case a picture is worth a thousand words.

Consider creating some good written work to take to the interview. Do not just hand this work over without comment but point out why you believe it to be good work. If you bring an old example of your written work, of course you should make sure the document doesn't contain confidential or sensitive information. Apart from the moral question, that would make it difficult if you are later asked about your ability to keep things confidential and/or secure.

Let's look at a sample answer to a very general question about communication:

> *'One of the selection criteria is communication skills. Do you feel that you have good communication skills?'*

You would be lucky to get the question in such a broad, easy form. Answering this question, 'Yes, I do', is not good enough. (It's hard to imagine anyone answering, 'No, I do not.')

A good answer would be:

> *'I believe I have good communication skills, both oral and written. I am always able to make myself understood in all situations, whether I am speaking to senior management or people from the factory floor. On occasion I have spoken to groups of up to a hundred people. I have also written some important reports which I have been commended on. I have brought a copy of one along to demonstrate this. All in all, I believe that communication skills are one of my strengths.'*

This is not a bad answer. It's just not a very good answer. It does mention a broad use of the skill—'from management to the factory floor'. It does mention some achievements—'... speaking to large groups, ... some important reports ...'—but it is not very conversational, and it does little other than deliver the basic information requested.

A better answer would be:

'I believe that good communication skills are important for good business; no, more than that, good communication skills <u>are</u> good business.

'I am a good communicator in most of the forms that communication takes place. I can converse well with a broad range of people from customers through to suppliers (hopefully with interviewers). Internally I have to deal with the factory floor people right through to senior management, indeed I have good friends from both places. On a daily basis, I have to communicate on a one-to-one basis, or sometimes with small groups and sometimes large groups of up to a hundred or more. This may be speaking to the people or writing to them.

'It seems to me that the key to good communications is to know or find out about the people you are communicating with and adjust the pitch accordingly. I would speak differently to a group of visiting students than I would to a group of visiting suppliers. I would word a letter of demand more formally than a memo to all staff about this year's Christmas party.

'I know that sounds obvious but I get frustrated sometimes by people who don't have that flexibility.

'Good communication is about access and understanding. It doesn't matter if the speech or the letter is technically correct if the people it is intended for do not understand it, or it is not communicated in a form that makes them want to understand it.

'I have brought along some reports which I believe are good examples of my written work; I will leave them with you so you can consider them at your leisure.

'The best example I have of my spoken communications is that two years ago we were involved in an unfortunate industrial dispute. I was not directly involved in the dispute but at the height of that dispute both sides asked me to help mediate, which I was able to do successfully. I am proud of the fact that both sides approached me.'

This answer makes all the good points that the previous answer made, but in addition it has comment, it puts over a better sense of achievement, and most importantly it has a sense of the philosophy behind good communication.

Because the examples of good answers that I am using are longer than the poor answers, don't fall into the trap of thinking that a long answer is a good answer. Some of the worst answers are long, rambling waffle. An answer should be just long enough to include all the necessary components, one of which is selling yourself.

Appearance

Appearances are vital. Interviewers often fall into the trap of judging a book by its cover; they shouldn't, but they do. Opinions are formed in the first few minutes of an interview, and appearance is a significant influence. What are the components of appearance? There are two: dress, including jewellery and grooming, and deportment.

Dress is not usually a major factor in the decision-making process; of course it could be, it's just that most people turn up to an interview wearing clothes, jewellery, and hairstyles that are within the expectations of the interviewers. Your minimum aim at an interview should be to satisfy the interviewers' expectations. Dress becomes a major factor only when you dress outside the expectations of the interviewers. There are always some people who do this, but it is surprising how many of them don't realise that they are doing so. There are three rules when it comes to clothes, jewellery and hairstyles:

1. They must reflect generally accepted current fashion standards.

2. They must be comfortable.

3. They must be appropriate.

If it is not possible to reconcile the first of these two rules, that is, if you can't feel comfortable wearing the current acceptable fashion, then you will have to learn how to do so, even if it means suffering graciously, because, of the three rules, reflecting current fashion is the most important.

Most of us know that it is possible to underdress for an interview. Usually, however, underdressing is only done by people who are deliberately building in an excuse for failure. Most people turn up looking as though they have made an effort to present themselves in a professional manner, which is exactly the image that you want to create.

It is also possible to overdress for an interview. Looking like a fashion model is fine if you are being interviewed for a job in a fashion house, but otherwise it is probably over the top. Do not look like the chief executive officer unless you are going for the chief executive's job. As long as you are still reflecting current standards I would advise you to err on the side of conservatism.

Current generally accepted fashion, need not be expensive. Yes, it may mean new if you have not bought any clothes for a while, but it is not necessary to spend a million dollars to look a million dollars. Remember the classics—the crisp white shirt or blouse and the polished black shoes—are generally accepted fashion. The white shirt, for both men and women, was accepted fashion thirty years ago and probably will be in thirty years time.

For men, the easiest indicator of fashion is your tie. Ties vary greatly from season to season; make sure you are wearing this season's. After ties comes the cut and then colour of your jacket and pants. Take a look around—what are other men wearing? Don't take your cue from men at work, because once you have a job there is often no need to continue updating your image. Look at men who are continually being assessed on their appearance, such as sales representatives and real estate agents.

For women, the demands of fashion are much harder to meet. Women need to be aware of fabrics, and have to contend with a broader array of colours, cuts and the use of accessories. It is often easiest and of most value to buy a basic outfit in one of the classic colours, such as navy. As with men, you should look around and make sure you are up to date, but don't overdo it.

Besides underdressing and overdressing there is simply wrong dressing. I learned this lesson the hard way. Some time ago I was coaching someone who was looking for a job in a company's purchasing office. James had been a purchasing officer for several years, and had left his job to start his own business with other members of his family. He had recently sold the business and was looking for a position similar to the one he had left.

James was confident and articulate, with good skills and a good work history. He was also very quick at absorbing the interview training; in short, he was highly employable, and I was sure that he wouldn't have more than three interviews before gaining employment.

Three interviews came and went, so did five and seven, with no job offers. I was surprised. In his line of work interviews did not come every week, and by now nearly six months had passed. I invited James over again for some more coaching. He seemed to remember what we had gone over earlier, and I was at a loss as to why he hadn't been successful. Another four interviews came and went, still with no job offer. By now I was getting worried; it looked as if James would be my first major failure. I also began to feel embarrassed because I had boasted to James that I would have him back at work in no time.

James was also worried, but he put his failure down to employers not liking the fact that he had left the profession to start his own business in another field. I was sure this wasn't the case, as I had helped James with a set of words to explain that situation. I felt certain the problem was somewhere else. James gained another interview and, in desperation, I asked him to call past my place on his way home from the interview and tell me exactly what he had been asked and how he had answered.

As soon as he arrived at my place the puzzle was solved: he looked dreadful. I knew James had never been particularly fashion-conscious, but I had presumed that he had a set of interview clothes that were passable. Boy, was I wrong! When he arrived at my place he looked as if he had dressed himself in the dark out of the wardrobe for a 1950s musical. He had on a brown, pin-striped sports coat which had very wide lapels, a blue business shirt with a wide yellow tie, blue slacks and brown polished shoes.

Of course it should not matter, within reason, what you wear at an interview. What you wear and your ability to do a job are two completely separate things. But the instant I saw James not only did I know why he wasn't getting the jobs, but I was pretty sure he was also the butt of many post-interview jokes.

I questioned James about his dress and I couldn't believe my ears. He assured me that he had been successful in the same clothes fifteen years earlier, when he had got his first job. His 'interview clothes' had been hanging in his wardrobe ever since! I explained that times and fashions had changed over fifteen years.

The post-script is that James went to his next interviews in some of my clothes, and gained a position at his third attempt. Coincidence? I think not.

The James story is a good illustration of the importance of reflecting current dress standards. By his own standards James was making an effort to go to the interview dressed smartly; he was after all wearing a jacket, shirt and tie. James is not alone in what I would call the 'brown sports coat syndrome' for men or the equivalent for women.

Recently one of the older men attending a course I was running was wearing a brown sports coat. This worried me. Should I mention the brown sports coat syndrome? Would it be rude to do so? In the end I decided that it would be rude to everyone else not to mention it, so I went ahead, with some trepidation. As soon as I finished, the man concerned stood up and said 'Philip I wish to differ. I am a university lecturer, and this is current fashion for university lecturers.' He was right too, down to the leather elbow protectors. There is always an exception that proves the rule.

From time to time I am asked by community groups to speak at seminars for older job seekers. It is very common to be approached at these seminars by people saying that they are a 'young fifty-two' or a 'young forty-eight', when they are making a statement with their dress that they are old-fashioned. Age may well be a state of mind but it can certainly be emphasised in the way you dress.

The problem with dated clothes is that they are taken as a signal that your work practices and ideas will also be dated, and that you won't be able to move with the times.

On the other hand, if you are the sort of person who prides themselves on being at the cutting edge of fashion, blunt yourself for the interview. Once you have won the position and proven yourself in the job then you can go back to making a fashion statement.

The second dress rule is that clothes must be comfortable. It is important to be comfortable in two ways: mentally and physically. It's no good wearing new shoes if they give you blisters and you limp to the interview, or squeezing into a dress if you're worried that it may split when you sit down. It's no good wearing a shirt collar that is so tight that it threatens to cut off your circulation and makes your face perpetually red. You must be physically comfortable in the clothes you wear.

Mentally, you must also feel at ease with the clothes you are wearing. It's no good going to an interview with clothes that you feel are just not you. And if you are very comfortable but not reflecting current standards, then you are doing yourself no favours.

I was coaching Susan for a position as a field biologist. She was passionate about rare native plants, and had gained some experience in this field on student placements and in voluntary positions. She told me that she was very nervous at interviews, and always 'messed them up'. I found this hard to believe because she was so confident and personable.

Positions in field biology are not that common and so I could not afford to learn where Susan was going wrong by trial and error. I questioned her in some detail about her previous interviews, including asking her what she wore. 'The usual interview stuff,' she replied.

On further questioning, 'the usual stuff' turned out to be quite formal: shoes with heels, stockings, a dress, handbag, painted fingernails and make up. What is wrong with this? Nothing necessarily, it's just that it didn't strike me as the kind of attire that Susan would be comfortable in. She agreed:

'I hate it. I never wear those type of clothes except at interviews.'

'Why do you wear them at interviews?'

'Because they are the best clothes I've got and you have to dress up at interviews.'

Susan went for her next interview in a pair of dress slacks, a shirt and flat shoes. She felt much more comfortable, and she did much better. She had been so uncomfortable in her previous interview clothes that it had affected her performance, and I'm sure it affected the interviewers. They must have looked at Susan in her office outfit and wondered if she really was suited to camping out and hands-on field biology.

This story leads me to the third dress rule: it must be appropriate. Susan's interview attire would have been appropriate for many office positions, but was not necessarily so for a field biology interview. I believe her attire was not appropriate. Are there clear rules on appropriate dress? Jeans may be worn to an interview at a jeans shop, but not many other places, except perhaps for labouring or unskilled positions, but even then I would make sure they were in good condition, clean, and worn with a neat shirt.

Some people think that you should wear to the interview the clothes you would wear on the job. This is not necessarily a good rule. Interviewees are expected to make an effort, to demonstrate that they really want the job, and part of this effort is dressing up. You can see this when there are interviews being held for internal promotions. What most interviewees wear to the interview will have no resemblance to the clothes they wore the day before, or will wear the day after. They're 'dressed-up' for the interview.

For most unskilled and semi-skilled work interviews, I would advise men to wear a pair of slacks with a crease in them, an open neck shirt, and a jumper if it is cold. Women could wear similar clothes but could also wear a simple dress or skirt.

For base-level office positions through to first-level supervisor positions men should wear a jacket and tie with a pair of dress slacks. Wearing a suit at this level would be overdressing. Women should wear a neat, conservative dress, or a skirt with a blouse and jacket. Unfortunately, I would advise you strongly not to wear slacks because—not in all cases but enough to matter—women applying for base-level positions through to first-level supervisor positions do better in skirts than in slacks.

The rules for base-level office positions also apply to any jobs where there is significant public contact. This means not only all sales positions, but also service trades or labouring positions where there is public contact. Even if you will be wearing overalls all day on the job, you should go to the interview in a jacket and tie, or a skirt and jacket if there is any public contact involved.

For senior supervisors or above in any occupation, or for professional positions, there is only the suit for both men and women. Interestingly, for women at this level the suit can be a pants suit though this isn't acceptable at the base-level position. It also isn't acceptable when applying for jobs in the law industry which still prefers skirts. Men should save their three-piece suits for very senior positions.

I am often asked if there are any particular colours which should or shouldn't be worn at an interview. My advice is to be guided by prevailing standards. If you are wearing a tie, wear only a plain white shirt, it is by far the safest choice. For women, avoid wearing all black, as for some strange and probably chauvinistic reason all black is still taken as a sign of being a *femme fatale*.

Keep jewellery to a conservative minimum, take the stud from your nose and if you are a man, from your ear. Hairstyles should be conservative, so avoid the orange rinse until the day after you have the job, and make sure that hair is away from your face. For men, shorter hair is still better than longer.

In giving this advice I can't help feeling that I am supporting attitudes which need to become more flexible. Making changes from within is easier than from outside, so if you agree, make sure when you reach a position of influence you do your part to bring about that change.

Deportment is closely linked to body language and therefore has been covered in detail in that section. It is important to keep your back straight and your head up, which will prevent you from slouching, which never gives a positive impression.

Honesty

Honesty is a very important selection criterion and yet it is a very difficult factor to judge. The question, 'Are you honest?', would surely bring only one answer, which is not, 'No I'm not actually, but I'm working on it.' Even leaving a ten-dollar note on the floor of the foyer for each interviewee would result in it being returned each time, as the interviewees displayed their honesty.

Most interviewers don't enquire directly about the interviewee's honesty, relying instead on the overall impression they get from the answers to other questions. But just because honesty is not directly questioned at an interview, don't think that you can afford to leave it to the interviewers' subjective approach. You must raise it as an issue, both directly and indirectly.

The easiest way to give the impression of honesty indirectly is to humbly admit some fallibility once or twice during the interview. For some reason there seems to be a strong link between the perceptions of humility and honesty. Humility may be shown by saying something like, 'I had trouble adjusting in the first place, but after a while ...', or 'The main thing I had to learn, and quickly, was ...'

It is also important to display honesty directly if you have the opportunity. The easiest way to do this is if you are asked, 'What are your strengths?'

One of the best strengths you can have is honesty. I will discuss how to respond to the strengths and weaknesses question later (page 136), but for now let's consider the use of honesty as one of your strengths. What is the worst way you can express honesty as a strength?: by including 'honesty' in among a list of other memorised qualities. Some interviewees run through their strengths in the same way that they refer to them on their résumés: 'I'm hardworking, conscientious, loyal, honest,' etc.

This is still poor, but somewhat better:

> *'One of my strengths that I am proud of is my honesty. I am very honest, it is something that is important to me. Another strength would be ...'*

This is the most common way that interviewees discuss their strengths. You need to do more than say, 'I believe that I am honest'; you need to expand your definition of honesty and express your own philosophy on what honesty means in a work sense. Here are a number of ways of doing this:

> *'... and one strength that I am proud of is honesty. I am very honest, not just in terms of not stealing, or handing in property that I find, although both of those things are important, but in the broader aspects of honesty.'*
>
> *'My word is important to me. If I say that something will be done by a certain time, you can rest assured that it will be done or that something well outside my control delayed it.'*
>
> *'To me honesty is about punctuality. If I say I will be at a certain place at a certain time then I have an obligation to be there at that time.'*
>
> *'To me honesty is about a fair day's work for a fair day's pay.'*
>
> *'A pet hate of mine is when people I work with take the day after a public holiday off sick to extend the long weekend. Honesty is about reliability.'*

Of course you shouldn't use all these statements at each interview, but you can select one or two, and perhaps add one of your own.

There is one proviso in raising honesty as an issue at an interview: your non-verbal communication must support your statement. Of course, if you are being interviewed for a position at Shonk and Shonk, tax consultants to the criminal bourgeoisie, then perhaps honesty might not be seen as such a virtue, and inventiveness might rate more highly.

Honesty doesn't have to be the first strength that you mention, but it does have to be on your list somewhere. Make sure that you include it in your interview answers in both direct and indirect ways.

Stability

Stability is one of those factors on which some interviewees mark themselves harder than the interviewers do. People have come to see me and pay a coaching fee just to ask how they could hide a period of unemployment. Some people are embarrassed by a lengthy period of unemployment. They carry their unemployment like a weight on their shoulders and it affects their self-esteem. Remember that if this weight is carried into the interview it will affect your performance. Often your attitude to your unemployment is more damaging to your chances than the period of unemployment itself.

It's true that stability is an important factor but this doesn't mean staying in each position for a long period. The days that our grandparents knew, when people would get a gold watch for twenty-five years of continuous service, have largely gone. It is far more common now for people to have broken work histories, and to change employers, occupations and industries. On the whole employers accept periods of unemployment more easily than they used to. Moreover, many employers realise that good people can be out of work for some time.

What is still important about your work history, though, is that you can logically explain it. Changing positions is not a bad thing, and periods of unemployment are not necessarily hindrances to gaining work, as long as you have a good reason for them. **Before you go into an interview you should know exactly how you will explain your work history when asked.**

There is only one acceptable reason for changing jobs by choice, and that is to seek advancement in your career. You may have wanted the new job because it offered more to learn, because it had greater or different responsibilities, or because it gave you new insight into the occupation or industry. All these reasons suggest that changing jobs made you a better employee and so hold some value for the current interviewer.

Reasons that are not well accepted for voluntarily changing jobs include:

more money

closer to home

felt like a change

The only good reason for leaving a job without another good job to go to, is that you were involuntarily laid off. The organisation you were with was reducing its staffing levels due to a process that was outside your control, and that does not reflect badly on the standard of your work.

Reasons for such processes may include:

poor sales due to the recession

currency fluctuations

dumping of imports

technological advancements

major restructuring of the organisation

organisation went out of business

If it is possible to include yourself as a victim of a 'last on, first off' employment policy with one of these reasons, all the better.

Poor reasons for leaving a job with no job to go to include:

personality clash

got offered a good package to leave

change of management

disciplinary reasons

pay dispute

Even if you left because of a genuine personality clash, you would be better off using a different reason if one was available. People who have personality clashes often make a habit of having them time and again, and even if yours was the first time ever and not your fault, it will still raise doubts in the minds of the interviewers. The only time to raise a personality clash is if the person that you clashed with was someone known for bastardry throughout the industry, including by these interviewers. In that case the clash might even be of benefit to you.

A good explanation for a period of unemployment is:

> *'When I first heard that the average length of unemployment for people in my position was eight months I was conceited enough to think that it would not apply to me. I have since learned the hard way that there are some good people unemployed for some time.'*

This answer will probably work unless you exceed the average length of unemployment for people in your category. If this is so, you may need to become a little more creative about what you have done with your time.

Other good answers include:

> *'I have been in the fortunate position to be able to completely renovate my period home, which is something I've had a desire to do for many years. However, now that that project is finished I am keen to get back to work.'*
>
> *'I have been in the fortunate position of being able to indulge myself in travel. It has been a life-long ambition to travel more, and I thoroughly enjoyed it, but now it is time to go back to achieving.'*

For travel or renovation you may substitute other hobbies or ambitions. Sometimes starting and running your own business can cover a period of unemployment, as can working in a friend's or a family business. If you use one of these reasons, you have to have a good reason for wanting to return to mainstream employment again. An answer which I have found particularly effective for people who have started their own business but prefer to go back to work in a larger organisation is:

> *'When I first had the idea that I would start my own business I was under the impression that it would be an exciting challenge, that the responsibility would be greater, that it would be a time of personal growth. In the start there were some elements of truth in these thoughts but over time it has become boring, it runs like clockwork and there is just not the range of issues that arise in a larger organisation.*

'Added to this the relationships that I make with customers stay on a professional level and there is not the closeness and camaraderie that I am used to. I miss working as part of a team. In short, starting my own business/consultancy was a romantic idea, and while it can be measured as a financial success and I have learned some new skills, I am not suited to it and I look forward to returning to the bigger picture which is available in larger organisations such as this one.'

Don't worry that your previous work history has to be exactly accounted for and that all the dates have to match up to complete a jigsaw picture. For the vast majority of employers, near enough is good enough, and many people run jobs into each other and omit some short-term jobs or short periods of unemployment without trouble. This is because, as stated earlier, interviewers are more concerned with what was learned than how long you were there, provided there is not a pattern to your work history which indicates irresponsibility.

Some sections of our community carry the weight of employment stability more heavily than others. I used to be an amateur athlete and one of my training partners, David, was a Koorie. David had a job and was also putting himself through night school to gain tertiary qualifications.

A position came up in the organisation that I worked for. I thought David was suitable for it and I encouraged him to apply. I did so for two reasons: I thought he was good for the job, and it paid ten thousand dollars a year more than he was earning. David said he would think about it.

Two days later David said he would not apply because:

'I have only been in my current position for eighteen months and if I leave now they will say that my people do not stay in jobs and will be less inclined to employ them.'

I have never felt the need to stay in a job because leaving might create a bad impression of white people.

A young woman was part of a small group I was coaching. She never paid attention, and I wondered why she had bothered to come. At the end of the session she stayed until everyone else had left. She burst into tears:

'But how do I go for an interview? I've been unemployed for nearly two years. How do I explain that? I feel so worthless.'

I immediately understood why she hadn't been paying attention. Here was a person who carried her unemployment like a weight around her neck. It was destroying her self-esteem. I said, 'But you have been employed.' She looked at me through her tears as though I had not heard or was stupid.

> *'I've been unemployed for nearly two years,' she said more loudly.*
> *'No you haven't,' I disagreed again, 'you have had a job looking after young children for a number of your neighbours. It is a job you have enjoyed, but now the children are of school age so you have to look for other work.'*

She looked at me while she considered what I had said. 'My neighbours would say that if I asked them to. It's true, I do a lot of baby sitting.'

> *'If they weren't the sort of people who would support you in that story I would have suggested relatives.'*

She went away with a large smile on her face. The whole session had been worthwhile for her because of that one answer. I just wish she had paid attention to the rest of the session.

Enthusiasm

Everyone knows that it is important at interviews to be seen as enthusiastic. However, the level of enthusiasm and the way in which it manifests itself must change depending on the job. If you are being interviewed for a junior trainee position, enthusiasm may be one of the key selection criteria. If you are being interviewed for a senior manager's position, enthusiasm is still on the agenda but is likely to rate below other factors.

As a junior your enthusiasm needs to know no bounds, you can be as enthusiastic as a puppy-dog. Appearing this enthusiastic when interviewing for a manager's position would be detrimental, as it would be viewed as immature. I learned this lesson the hard way.

The first time that I was interviewed for a manager's position I was placed second by the interview panel. This sounds better than it actually was, as there were only two people interviewed. My perception was that I had done quite well at the interview and I was disappointed. I asked to see the interview write-ups. The report sang my praises throughout, containing only one detrimental comment:

> *'The panel was not convinced that Philip's boyish enthusiasm could be maintained over time.'*

What a velvet put-down. For 'boyish enthusiasm', read 'Philip was immature'. If the interviewers decide that you are immature, it is irrelevant how well you do in the rest of the interview; they will always find a reason not to give you the job.

The way that enthusiasm is displayed at an interview should go through a change from personal enthusiasm for base-level positions:

'I'm so keen to work in this area', or *'I can't wait to start, there is just so much to learn.'*

through enthusiasm for the job at supervisor level:

> *'This job can achieve so much more if it can become the two-way link between more senior management and the operators, if it can collect and pass ideas and suggestions upwards as well as downwards.'*

to enthusiasm for what can be achieved by the organisation at more senior levels:

> *'I am sure that if I can enthuse my people with the same vision of what can be achieved, and correctly harness their energies, then together we can start the snowball rolling and have it build and build until the results that we end up with as commonplace were once only considered in our hopes.'*

Remember that introducing your enthusiasm directly is only part of the story, and it must be supported by your demeanour in the rest of the interview.

Leadership

Leadership is another area where interviewees make life hard for themselves, particularly those who have not been supervisors. There is a general perception that if you haven't been a supervisor, the only way you can demonstrate leadership is by being or having been the captain of a sporting team. What a nonsense! My memory of sporting captains is mainly that they were bigger, louder, or better at the sport than the rest of us. Leadership qualities had little to do with their selection.

Of course if you happen to be or have been a captain, this is not a bad thing to raise at an interview. If you do, it is better to suggest that the captaincy was decided on a vote from the players rather than as an appointment from administrators. The former is more indicative of peer group support and hence leadership qualities.

If you haven't been a supervisor or a captain then what is needed is a set of words that indicate your natural leadership qualities. A set of words that I have used with some success in coaching graduates looking for their first job is:

'In my family and among my friends I am recognised as the person to see if you have a problem and need some advice. I am not suggesting that I am a sort of Dear Jane columnist, it is just that if you are seen to be in control of your own life and handling any problems that arise, then other people notice this and seek your advice and direction.

'I think that is the secret of true leadership; to be seen to be doing the right thing and being successful. Leadership is about "do as I do, not just do as I say".'

Being a supervisor or manager, is not enough to demonstrate leadership qualities. You will still have to describe your philosophy of leadership and the lessons that your experience has taught you.

Until recently most organisations recognised leadership only when it was shown during a crisis. Managers who could step in when there was a major problem and make the necessary decisions to overcome it were seen as leaders. Recently, however, companies have come to realise that too many managers of this type create an imbalance, and in fact some of these managers subconsciously help to create problems so that they can step in and cover themselves with glory by providing the solutions. Consequently, there is growing recognition of the value of another type of manager, the one who avoids having a crisis in the first place by careful planning, monitoring, and acting early when problems arise.

This information can be used at interviews, usually in response to a question on leadership or management style. The answer might be:

'Leadership alone is inconsequential; what is important is the type and quality of leadership that senior people in organisations give, the setting of the mood and culture within an organisation. To me leadership is about "do as I do, not just do as I say". It is about action, words and philosophy. It is about leading by example, not just in the big things but in the small decisions that are made all day every day.

'I believe that in the past too many organisations have given too much credit to crisis managers and not given enough credit to those quieter, less obvious managers who plan well, monitor, supervise closely and avoid problems altogether. Either this or get to problems when they are small and keep them that way.

'I don't believe the two types are mutually exclusive and certainly a good manager should have skills in both areas. Of the two I believe I am closer to the second type of manager, the planning, avoiding problems type. I am proud of being like this and intend to try and stay this way It may not cover me in glory as much as the high profile managers who continually

step into the breach and save the day but I believe that in avoiding problems in the first place I am just as valuable to the company.'

Team Work

Team work was not on our list of selection factors, but is a factor that is taken into account by many interviewers and so you should take a little time to consider how best to give the impression that you are a good team player.

Team work is a little like honesty, in that a direct question regarding your ability to work as part of a team would surely bring about only a positive response. The best way to handle team work questions is different now to what it was ten years ago.

In the 1980s many industrial communities moved from single task jobs to the age of 'multi-skilling'. Team work became one of the catch-cries of this restructuring process, and was rated very highly by interviewers. It became a euphemism for flexibility, for workers being willing to take on a broader range of jobs and responsibilities than they had before. During this period, describing yourself as a team player was in effect giving your support to these new work arrangements and was mandatory at interviews.

It is still important to demonstrate that you are a team player, but not as much as it was during the restructuring process. One of the reasons for this, I believe, is that some organisations and workers took team work a little too far. The team was responsible for everything, individuals for nothing. When something went wrong who was responsible? Not me. Not me. Not me either. It was the team. The team became a convenient scapegoat for anything that went wrong. A cartoon on this subject would show a supervisor asking the workers in a team, 'Is this your signature?' and having each person deny it. Consequently, it is now possible to be too much of a team player.

The best responses to team work questions these days offer certain qualifications. This set of words has had success among many people I've coached:

> *'Team work is important to me, in fact I don't think I could work as effectively in an area where there was no team work, where people worked as islands and did not support each other, particularly through problems and peak periods. However, I think that team work can be taken too far and some people can use team work to avoid personal responsibilities.*
>
> *'I like to work as part of a team but within that team I like*

to be clear about what my area of responsibility is. Sometimes the best contribution that I can make to the team is to have everyone in the team relax in the knowledge that I will do my job to the best of my ability, and if anyone needs help then they know that they only have to ask, and importantly they should know that if I need help I will ask. That to me is a good example of team work.'

If you are being interviewed for a supervisor's or manager's position and you are asked, 'How would you encourage team work in your work place?', be sure to include something similar to the above answer in your response.

Chapter 9

THE INTERVIEW

First Stages

You may be surprised that you are so far into a book primarily about interviews before you get to a chapter named 'The Interview'. But it shows how much preparatory work has to be done before you actually get to the interview itself.

Here is a scenario. You have an interview tomorrow. Tonight you are a little anxious and you probably don't sleep well. The morning comes and your normal routine is disrupted as you get ready. You put on a set of clothes that you have designated your 'interview' clothes. They aren't what you usually wear, and friends who see you ask, 'Going for an interview?' You feel that even people who don't know you, know where you are going, and give you that knowing smile of sympathy.

You worry so much about being late that you arrive too early. You have a coffee while taking a last look at your notes. When you finally get there the receptionist knows you are the next 'bunny' for interview, and gives you the sympathetic smile that you are starting to recognise. The receptionist dislikes interviews too.

Interviewers, like doctors and dentists, seem to be always running late. It frustrates me that organisations still allow only half an hour for each interview, including the after-interview discussion. It is just too short a time, and as a result you sometimes have to wait twenty to thirty minutes before your interview starts. The receptionist tries to start a conversation but gives up, as you are too preoccupied. She offers you a cup of coffee instead, but you decline because you are too nervous.

After fifteen minutes the door opens and someone comes out. You get up, only to realise that it is a rival, who has just finished their own interview. You sit down again, and study the rival to see how they look. If they look confident you say to yourself, 'Damn, they must have gone well.' If they look harrowed you say, 'Damn, it must be a difficult interview.' You nod to your rival. 'Good luck', you say hollowly to each other.

Five minutes later the door opens again and this time it is a person who is obviously an interviewer. You start to stand up, but the interviewer waves at you to be seated. 'We're not ready yet. Sorry to keep you waiting, but we're running late,' they say, stating the obvious. You worry that you looked silly being caught between standing and sitting, and notice that the interviewer said 'we', indicating more than one interviewer: a panel. You wonder how many. Two? Three? Hopefully no more than three.

Remember that the interview starts the minute the first interviewer sets eyes on you. Many interviewees have been sitting waiting for twenty minutes or more, but the second that they stretch out and yawn an interviewer pops out and catches them in an awkward pose.

Ten minutes after disappearing back into the interview room the interviewer reappears, this time with a welcoming smile. You get to stand all the way up.

A new dilemma is felt at this point. Do you shake hands, or let the interviewer make the first move? My advice is to take the lead and shake hands. By leading you are making a statement about your openness and friendliness. You also avoid the embarrassment of having your right hand move backwards and forwards, as if sawing wood, as you watch for the signals from the interviewer. Also you will avoid putting your hand out, and having the interviewer grip and shake your fingers. Nothing dents your confidence more at the start of an interview than giving the 'wet fish' handshake.

Take the lead in shaking hands whether you are male or female, whether the interviewer is male or female, whether one of you is older than the other, whether one of you has a different skin colour or is from a different culture from the other. If someone clearly doesn't want to shake hands as may be the case amongst some cultural groups, smile and nod to show you understand and are not offended. Never shake hands in an aggressive or authoritative way. Crushing bones in a vice-like grip impresses few people.

As you shake hands, hold your chin high, get good eye contact, smile and say, 'Pleased to meet you', or 'Hello David', 'Hello Adele', or 'Hello Mr Scott', according to how the interviewer has introduced themselves. Never forget the likeability factor.

Repeat this process as you are introduced to other panel members. Go out of your way to shake hands, even if some panel members are seated away from where you will sit.

Then, as everyone is settling down to start the interview, I would do two more things:

1. First, I would take some notes from my briefcase and say something like, 'I have some notes here that I may refer to if I have a mental block.' I would then place the notes within easy reach, either on a desk or table if one is provided, or the floor.

   Many interviewees are in the habit of taking briefcases, satchels or at least manila folders into interviews. Often these are just fashion accessories, and are only for show. After the job-seeker has left the room briefcase unopened, the interviewers may joke to each other, 'What was in that briefcase? A newspaper and an apple?' The rule is, if you take a briefcase or some such into an interview then you must open it and take something out of it. If you take out some notes and/or a copy of your application and résumé, the advantage is that you can look at them if you do have a mental block, as Kevin did in the example mentioned earlier.

   But beware: if you use notes extensively, you will lose points from your overall interview rating. Still, I would rather lose points than have a mental block. Also, with the security blanket of your own notes handy, you are less likely to have a mental block.

   It is perfectly acceptable to use notes to clarify some detail that is asked for. For example, 'How much budget did you spend on accommodation last financial year?', 'From memory it was one hundred and sixty-five thousand dollars; I have the figure here. No, it was one hundred and seventy-five thousand dollars.' You will not lose points for looking up points of clarification in that way. Interviews are not tests of memory.

   Nobody I have coached has ever reported back that they have had a problem with taking notes into an interview. If you are not comfortable taking out notes, take out copies of your application and résumé on the pretext they may be referred to at some stage. It is handy to have a few spare copies of each in case they are referred to and not every panel member has a copy.

2. The second thing I suggest if you are a man is to take off your jacket and roll up your shirt sleeves. I would do this for some very good reasons. As I mentioned earlier, interviewing can be quite tiring and difficult for the interviewers, especially if the interviewees are overly nervous or poor in their performance. It is unnerving when an interviewee is asked a difficult question and shoots a pained and accusing look at the panel. At the start of an interview there is often some strain as the interviewers assess how hard or how easy this interview is going to be.

   By taking off your jacket and rolling up your sleeves you are trying to give three subconscious messages to the interviewers.

The first is, 'I am ready to start', a good signal to give. It is almost like saying, 'Let the games commence.' The second message is, 'I understand the roles here, it is your job to ask questions and mine to answer them. I accept this, with no hard feelings.' The third message is, 'I am prepared to work hard at this interview: it is important to me.'

All three messages can be signalled at the crucial early stage of first impressions by taking off your jacket and rolling up your sleeves. Of all the advice I give about interviews, this is the area that most bothers those I coach. I know it is a good thing to do, particularly in those formal panel interviews. I don't recommend it for the more informal one-to-one interviews where it would be over-the-top and silly; some discretion is needed. If you are not comfortable with it, or if you are a woman, or a man who does not wear a jacket and a shirt, think of another way of giving the same messages. Some of the women and men I have coached suggested just tugging at their shirt or jacket sleeves as they sat down, and have reported that this seemed to do the trick.

Once you sit down you should sit in the 'straight back, leaning forward position' with good eye contact, as mentioned in 'Body Language'. You are now ready to go.

The first questions are usually small talk, sometimes very small talk:

'Did you find a park?'
'Did you come on the train or by car?'
'Did you find the place OK?'
'Did you get caught in the rain?'

The interview and the assessment of you has started, and at the very least you should come out of the small talk 'neutral', that is, you are neither closer nor further away from winning the job. You would remain neutral by smiling and saying something like, *'Yes, thank you'*, or *'By car today.'*

Some people actually lose ground during the small talk. I remember asking one woman, *'Did you find a park OK?'* She replied, *'No, I didn't, I'm in a "no standing" spot. I'll have a ticket by the end of the interview.'* Why did she tell us this? Was she looking for the sympathy vote? Even if she was parked in a 'no standing' spot the answer should have been, *'Yes, thank you.'*

I remember asking one man, *'Did you get here OK?'* His reply was, *'No, actually; it is a bus and a train from my place to here and do you think they connect? I had to wait twenty-eight minutes between one and the other!'* Again the sympathy vote? The interviewers' response to this kind of answer is similar to yours when you ask someone, *'How are you?'* and are told of about four different ailments. You asked but you didn't really want to know.

At best, small talk could give you some gains. I remember asking one young man, *'Did you find the place OK?'* He replied, *'Yes, thank you, I am a little nervous about the interview and I didn't want to make it worse by being late today, so I drove past last night so I'd know exactly where to come.'* Immediately this young man has been able to demonstrate forward planning and attract attention to himself as a potential candidate.

Another thing he did which is a good idea at the start of an interview was to bring up the fact that he was a little nervous, this in effect saying, *'This interview is important enough to me to make me nervous.'* We are not nervous at interviews for jobs that we don't really want. *'I am a little bit nervous'*, if fitted naturally into the small talk, also gives you a little room to be excused if you do stumble due to nervousness during the first few questions.

This story is dear to me: I was coaching the young Indian man and I was explaining about the small talk. He said:

> *'Oh Philip, I think it is in this area that I have been making a mistake. Just last week I had an interview and the interviewer asked me if I smoked and I told him that I did not. I also went on to tell him that I do not eat meat. I do not eat anything with sugar added. I do not eat anything with salt added. I only eat natural products such as brown rice and vegetables.'*

If the interviewer was looking at Kumar and thinking, 'You look different, you sound different, you will not "fit in", Kumar's response was to in effect say, 'Yes, I look different, I sound differ-ent, and in fact I am very, very different. In fact I am probably more different than you even thought I was. I will almost certainly never "fit in".'

Kumar continued by saying to me, *'You see Philip, I thought the fact that I was such a pious man would impress them.'* Pious? When was the last time you heard 'pious' in a conversation?

I said, *'Kumar, not for you pious. From now on for you—pie and sauce.'* I coached him to say that he went to the football on Saturday and had a barbecue with his family on Sunday. Did he do either of these things? No. Should he have had to say either of these things? No. But if I know that interviewers are looking at Kumar and thinking, 'you look different, you sound different, you will not "fit in"', then I have to get Kumar to say, 'I look different, I sound different but underneath I am no different to you. My values are your values.'

Now Kumar is working. The last word should remain with him. He said, *'In India it is different. When we ask we really want to know.'*

Chapter 10

QUESTIONS AND ANSWERS

Why You?

The first real question that you are likely to be asked comes in a number of forms, but in essence it is 'why you?' It might be as direct as, 'Why should you get this job?', but other forms include:

'What brings you here today?'
'Why did you apply for the job?'
'What do you have to offer?'
'Why do you believe your background is relevant to this position?'

In its most aggressive form the question is:

'Why should you get this job ahead of the seven other people we are interviewing?'

A form of this question is usually asked first, because it is considered the question most likely to get applicants settled into the interview and speaking fluently. After all, if you can't speak coherently about something you know about—you—how will you answer the more difficult questions? But if it isn't asked first it is sometimes asked last, but it is the one question you will almost certainly be asked in one form or another. Even if you are not asked this question, the work you will do in preparing for this answer will be valuable throughout the interview. The answer is one of those that you should work out, write down and learn beforehand. Your response should be your strongest answer at the interview. But despite all this, the question is usually answered poorly. Let's look at a poor answer:

'I'd like to start the interview by asking you to tell us why you applied for this position.'

'Well, this job is the sort of job that I've been looking for. It's in the area of work where I have a great deal of experience. I have good skills and knowledge to offer in this area. I've always been interested in this type of work and I've been in this broad area of work since I left school. I have good references for my work in this area. I enjoy working in this area.

'I believe that this is a very reputable company that would be good to work for and would offer me the scope for advancement once I show what I'm capable of. I think that working here would be a challenge until I have proven myself, but I enjoy a challenge and perform well under those circumstances. I've been constantly searching the newspaper for this type of work and when I saw your advertisement I rang and made enquiries before applying to be sure that the job matched my range of skills. It checked out so I applied.'

If this reminds you of your own answer, don't be surprised, it is a fairly standard answer. A little more detail specific to the job or to the organisation may be added in some cases. It is not a bad answer in that it is standard, and therefore is no worse than the answer anyone else is giving. If eight people are being interviewed for the position the chances are that all eight will answer in a similar way. The problem is that it is no better than the answers of the other seven and, therefore, does not give you an advantage.

Most interviewees don't answer this question well because they do not believe it is a 'real' question. They think that it's a continuation of the opening small talk. They believe that the 'real' questions to follow will test their knowledge, skills and experience in some way. Most people really are locked into the belief that interviews are tests of memory. But make no mistake: this question *is* a real question and a good answer is important. The answer was poor, but it is not the worst possible answer. Consider:

'Because I'm a great accounts clerk, and you're looking for a great accounts clerk. That's why I applied for the job.'

I know that I suggested selling yourself for the job, but is this really selling? Would you buy anything from a person giving this answer? More relevantly, would you buy this person? Remember: we like people who are confident, but we dislike people who are conceited. It is answers like this that make interviewers wish that they had a button they could press to open a trapdoor and make certain interviewees disappear. There are answers, however, still worse than this:

'I need a job and this is a job I can do.'

It is not a good idea to mention your needs at interview unless there is no alternative or it is such a low-skilled, low-paying job that the desire to work is the major selection factor. Here is another poor reply:

'I didn't see the job; actually my mother saw it in the newspaper. She pointed it out to me and said, "Isn't that the type of work that you've been looking for?" I had a look and it was, so I applied.'

This was a real answer given to me at an interview some time ago from someone who, sadly, may still be looking for work.

Clearly there are better ways of answering the question, 'Why you?' The standard answer is a poor answer because it doesn't 'use' the question to full advantage. We know from previous chapters that what sells at an interview is wisdom, insight and understanding, and there are none of these in the standard answer.

For most jobs this question cannot be answered properly in under four to five minutes, and for jobs of any responsibility at all it cannot be answered in under five to ten minutes. To talk for five to ten minutes on any subject without waffling is difficult unless you have a clearly defined structure.

The answer to this question should come in four parts:

how you see the job
what the job needs
this is you
summary

The first thing to do, and the trick to answering this question well, is to allow you to broaden your answer. The way to do this depends on the way the question is asked. If it is, 'Why did you apply for this job?', your reply should start in the following way:

'Before I tell you why I applied I think it is important that you know how I see the job, because that, more than anything else, will explain why I applied.'

It is unlikely that you will receive any objections to this approach; no one coached ever has.

It is harder to turn around a directive than a question. If the interviewer says, 'Tell us about your background in relation to this job', try:

> *'It may be easier in talking about my background in relation to this job if I start with how I see the position first, and then how I see my background in relation to the position.'*

If you are asked to 'Tell us about the job as you see it', try:

> *'In telling you about the job I'd also like to include how I see myself in relation to the job.'*

This will usually present no problems.

Once you have opened the question to allow a broader answer the next thing to say, regardless of the job, is:

> *'It's an important position.'*

In saying this you are reflecting the interviewers' feelings about the position. They must feel that it is important; after all, they have taken the trouble to advertise and interview when they could have employed the first person who walked in off the street. If you are being interviewed for a key position in an organisation, then consider reflecting this at the start of your answer in this way:

> *'Before I tell you why I applied for the position I think you should know how I see the job because this in part will explain why I applied. It's obviously an important position ...'*

The next thing to do is to tell the interviewers of the wonderful things that could be achieved if the 'right' applicant was appointed to the job. What is at the heart of this job? Why does the organisation have this job? What is the scope for this job? In effect the idea is to steal the high ground in your view of the job.

It disappoints me how few people actually do this basic work in preparation for an interview. If you cannot articulate even to yourself how things would look if this job were done well, how can you present yourself as a person who can do the job well?

People sometimes come out of an interview and say, 'I didn't get the opportunity to tell them this, I didn't get the chance to tell them that.' Sometimes this is true, but more often the interviewee just didn't *see* the opportunity, didn't *take* the opportunity, didn't *make* the opportunity. Making opportunities starts with turning around the first question to suit your answer.

In turning the question around and saying how you see the job it is not merely a matter of repeating the duty statement or the advertisement back to the interviewers. Instead it is an opportunity to demonstrate your wisdom, insight and understanding of the job. The aim of stating how you see the job, is to have each of the interviewers feel that you speak their language even when what that means may not be entirely clear to them because it is 'hidden'. 'This person speaks my language' means 'likeability' and it indicates the thought, 'This person's views are similar to my own.'

Receptionist

A young woman I recently coached for a receptionist's job said this when asked the 'Why you?' question:

> *'Before I tell you why I applied for this position I'd like to start by telling you how I see it because this will in part explain why I applied.*
>
> *'For starters I believe that the receptionist position is very important to an organisation. The first contact that a client has with a company is often with the receptionist. It is important that this first contact leaves a good impression. At that stage the receptionist is the company, as far as the client is concerned; that is, the impression that the receptionist gives is the impression the client is left with of the whole company. I believe that the receptionist's job is to make every client feel that their custom is valued and appreciated.*
>
> *'I know that a receptionist is important because I recently changed dentists, not because my dentist wasn't good, but because the receptionist there was quite rude to me.*
>
> *'But the job of a receptionist is not only about being nice to people who walk through the door; there is also a role to play within the company. Not every enquiry that comes to the switchboard or the counter needs to be passed on. A good receptionist should know the company business well enough to know which enquiries can be handled at reception and which need to be passed on. If a receptionist does this well everyone else can relax and get on with their work without petty interruptions or worrying about missing out on leads at the reception desk.*
>
> *'The third part of being a receptionist is having other skills and being willing to do other duties when reception is quiet. I hate sitting around waiting for the phone to ring or people to come in.'*

This is a pretty good start to her answer to the question, 'Why did you apply for this position?' It covers the very heart of what being a receptionist is all about. But you will not read this on any duty statement or list of selection criteria. When I read out this response in my coaching, people smile and nod their heads in agreement as they recognise the 'heart' of the job of receptionist. Incidentally, the receptionist had not recently changed dentists, but it did add a nice touch to her answer, a touch she came up with on her own.

In talking about the job of receptionist in this way, I am sure that she had the interviewers constantly nodding their heads in agreement, which is exactly what you want them to be doing at an interview. All organisations want a receptionist who realises the value of clients and the relationship between reception and clients in the way that this answer indicated. This is an example of stealing the high ground, and the same technique can be applied to any position. Here are two examples:

Truck Driver

> 'Before I tell you why I applied for the position let me tell you how I see the job because that in part will explain why I applied. It is an important job. Many people underestimate the importance of a driver, but I see my role as an on-the-road representative of the company. That goes for both the customers that I deliver to and other road users. It's no good the company spending thousands of dollars presenting an image of being efficient and community conscious if the only part of the company that the public and the customers see is a scruffy, rude and lazy truck driver.
>
> 'It is the same with reliability. It is no good the factory breaking its neck to get an order out on time if the driver is not there to deliver it or is running late and misses a delivery or delivers it to the wrong people.'

Personnel Officer

> 'Before I tell you why I applied for this job let me tell you how I see the job because that in part will explain why I applied. Personnel Officer is obviously a key position in an organisation, and is central to the administration and smooth running of an organisation.
>
> 'Having said that, I have a personal belief that the more invisible a Personnel section is, the better. I say this because the only time most people think of Personnel is when there is a problem of some kind. It might be a problem with pay, or a problem with leave or an industrial relations problem. Such problems distract staff attention away from the real work of the organisation. Consequently if nobody is thinking of Personnel, then Personnel must be running pretty smoothly, and it is my responsibility as the Personnel Officer to bring this about.
>
> 'Secondly I think that a Personnel Officer has an important

role to play as an honesty broker within the organisation. The respect for the integrity of Personnel should be such that staff are inclined to ask for advice and guidance before small problems become large ones. Keeping molehills, molehills is, I believe, an important function of Personnel. To do this there has to be some sense of leadership, and it has to be "do as I do", not just "do as I say". The Personnel section has to have its own house in order. If the Personnel section is to give advice that is sometimes unpopular, people will be quick to say "People in glass houses should not throw stones."

'The third and final area that I see in the job is the proactive policy area. If the organisation is going to be dynamic and meet the constantly changing needs of the market place then it needs to have staffing policies and practices that are current and reflective of a modern workplace. It is my job as the Personnel Officer through the Personnel team to bring this about, and I'm talking about policies and practices in place as they are needed, not "after the event". I believe in being proactive, not reactive.'

Remember that I am not suggesting this exact set of words to you, unless of course you happen to be applying for one of the above jobs and have the same views about it as I do. **The important point is that at the start of the question you make room to talk about the position and give your views on the importance of the position and what it can achieve.** This is part one of the four-part answer.

The second part of the answer is to talk about the knowledge, skills and personal qualities that the position needs in order to achieve the goals that you have outlined in the first part of the answer. Do not fall into the trap of talking about yourself at this stage, although that is tempting; you will have the opportunity in part three. The second part of the answer for the three jobs might sound like this:

Receptionist

'A good receptionist needs certain skills and personal qualities. For starters they need to have a good appearance. I'm not talking about being a fashion model, but about a professional appearance which is in keeping with the image of the company. A good receptionist needs to be friendly and polite and have a genuine liking for people. The easiest way of demonstrating this is with a smile. But the reception area should not be a gossiping post either. I believe that you can be friendly but still professional.

'A good receptionist also needs to know how to use tact. Sometimes the client at reception cannot be seen when they turn up, particularly if they do not have an appointment. The client needs to be booked in at another time in such a way that they still feel that their business is important. I was working on reception once with another receptionist and he told a client, "He's too tied up to see you now, you will have to come back another time." The message was true but it could have been put more tactfully and professionally.

'Finally, a receptionist needs other skills which can be used when reception is quiet, particularly first thing in the morning and last thing at night.'

Truck Driver

'A good truck driver needs to have some manners, both on the road and with customers. A good driver has to be quick while at the same time being safe, and to have a flexible attitude. I've worked with some people who have said, "I drive, I don't load or unload", which I think is a nonsense. But most of all a driver needs to be reliable and punctual.'

Personnel Officer

'The role of the Personnel Officer is a demanding one and requires a broad range of knowledge and skills. Firstly, there is the bread and butter, the day-to-day administration of the personnel function, the pay and leave. The Personnel Officer needs to know the rules and the processes well, and also has to be able to do the work. I believe in getting my hands dirty and leading from the front whenever the opportunity allows.

'Then there is the honesty and integrity that I spoke about. It is not the sort of thing that people will believe just because you say that you have it. Honesty and integrity have to be proven over time and so a Personnel Officer has to be able to display these qualities in the day-to-day work with staff at all levels. Communication skills, both written and verbal, are crucial to the role of Personnel Officer.

'Finally a Personnel Officer has to have a good understanding of the company business in terms of the markets, the customers and the product. If this understanding can take in the history of the company and the industry, the current situation and, importantly, the future, then all the better. I believe that this in-depth knowledge is crucial to the development of personnel policies that are relevant and contribute to the ongoing competitiveness of the company.'

To give yourself further guidance and structure through the second part of the answer it sometimes helps, depending on the job that you are applying for, if you can sort what the job requires into three distinct areas:

1. technical skills;

2. personal skills;

3. administration skills (for some positions you may prefer to substitute management skills for administration skills).

Do not restrict yourself to just the technical skills. It would be a rare job that required technical skills and nothing else.

If you chose to do this, the introduction to the second part of your answer might begin in this way:

> *'To be successful in this position I believe that skills are needed in three distinct areas: technical skills, administration skills and personal skills. In the technical skills area I believe a person doing this job needs to know ...'*

The technical skills area is fairly self-explanatory, and whether you learned them through study or on the job, you should say enough to make it clear that you understand them.

Under administration or management skills, list such items as decision making, priority setting, standard setting and the current 'buzz words' such as 'just in time', 'benchmarking', or 'best practice'.

Under the umbrella of 'personal skills' should go the ability to get on with a wide range of people, to communicate, and to lead, if applicable to the position.

The third part of the answer is 'this is me'. Clearly the third part will be easier if the second part has been tailored to meet the skills, knowledge and personal qualities that you have. It is no good demonstrating that the job needs skills, knowledge and personal qualities that you will later show that you do not possess. Of course this would be foolish.

The third part of the three jobs might sound like this:

Receptionist

'I understand the importance of being a good receptionist. I realise the importance to the company of the clients who come in or ring up. I think I have a good professional appearance, and I have a good way with people, I am sure that each of my referees will support this. I understand the need for tact on occasion. I have bookkeeping and other clerical skills that can be utilised during the quiet periods.'

Truck Driver

'I am a good driver. I am safe and reliable and my driving record demonstrates this, as do my referee comments. I understand the importance of a good driver to the company, but most of all I am honest, reliable and punctual. I like to just get on with the job and do it; do it well so that people who rely on me can just get on with their own work.'

Personnel Officer

'I have a broad range of knowledge and skills. I am able to both operate and supervise manual and computer pay and leave systems. I gained this experience at Acme Corp and will be supported by my referees there.

'I am known and respected for my honesty. Again, anyone who has worked with me would attest to this but more importantly anyone working with me in the future will quickly come to know this. I understand the importance of leadership and of ethics in leadership in setting the culture within an organisation.

'I have good communication skills, both written and oral, and I have the ability to get on with and make friends with a wide range of people from the boardroom to the factory floor. I have brought along a copy of a major report that I was asked to submit while I was at Acme Corp to demonstrate my written communication skills. You will notice that some of the details are missing—that's because they are details that are confidential to Acme Corp and should remain that way. The report is on how to determine the comparative worth of employees in different parts of the organisation and following this report, Acme Corp streamlined a number of pay scales.

'Lastly I have a good understanding of this industry and its markets, and the factors which affect the market, both in a micro- and macro-economic sense. I believe that I can translate this understanding into personnel policies and procedures which reflect a professional, progressive organisation.'

The last part of the answer is the summary; whether or not this is needed will be determined by the length of the other parts of the answer. In the examples demonstrated, the truck driver would need only a closing sentence or so, but the receptionist and the personnel officer would need a true summary.

Receptionist

'In summary, I believe that I understand the importance of the receptionist position. I believe that I know the range of skills and knowledge that a receptionist needs and that I have the skills that would enable me to make a contribution to the efficiency of the company. That is why I applied for the position.'

Truck Driver

As the truck driver's answer was more concise than those of the receptionist or the personnel officer, no summary would be needed.

Personnel Officer

'In summary I believe that I have a full understanding of the broad role of the Personnel Officer. I have experience in the full range of duties from payroll and leave through to policy writing and delivery. I am aware of the need and role of a pro-active Personnel area that sets an example within the organisation. All of this experience is demonstrated on my résumé and will be supported by my referees. After careful consideration of what the job entails and matching my own skills to those needs, I believe that I can make a valuable contribution to this company. That is why I applied for this position.'

By now I believe that you should be able to see and recognise the structure and benefit of this answer. Yes, it is a formula reply, but there is nothing wrong with a formula as long as it works. The formula in this case only provides a structure; the words and beliefs about the job within that structure should be yours alone. Five different people at an interview could use this structure, yet each answer would be unique.

Compare the three examples of how to approach the answer to this question with the examples given earlier of poor and standard answers. The four-part way is clearly more impressive at an interview. It also has two other advantages:

1. It is usually asked first, and so falls within those first few minutes which are vital to that first impression.

2. It is the question you are almost assuredly going to get asked, and therefore you can compose an answer and learn it before the interview.

The only problem that I have come across with this answer is that sometimes you may get ahead of the interviewers. A list of questions may include 'Why did you apply for this position?' and later 'What skills do you think are necessary for this position?' If you answer the first question as suggested it will also encompass the answer to the second question. Most interviewers will recognise this and say something like:

> *'We had another question that we were going to ask which was, "What skills do you think the position needs?"*
> *However, you covered that in your first answer so we will go on with a different question.'*

However, some interviewers will be so pedantic that they will feel compelled to ask each applicant the same questions regardless of the previous answers. If you find yourself in that position do not get upset, just introduce your answer by saying, 'As I said in my earlier answer I believe that there are a number of skills and personal qualities needed in the position ...' and go on to paraphrase what you said earlier.

If you put all four sections of the answer together, in each of the jobs illustrated, you will see that it is quite an imposing reply. If you have not been answering in this way, it may even be a daunting answer. Now you will understand what I mean when I say you cannot answer this question in under five minutes for most jobs and five to ten minutes for jobs of any responsibility. Also, it is nearly impossible to come up with an answer like this on the spot, and this should demonstrate the importance of preparation.

As well as being an imposing answer this is quite a good answer. There is no doubt that this answer will be considered more impressive than the standard answer. The reason it is more impressive is that it contains some wisdom, insight and understanding and we have created a structure within the answer that allows us to do that. If you were to use this answer, let's say for the Personnel Officer, it would contain enough detail for the 'Why you?' question but could lead on to a number of other questions, such as:

> *'You mentioned your experience in computer pay systems—which systems do you have experience with?'*
>
> *'You mentioned the importance of the Personnel Officer's position being an honesty broker—how do you envisage this would work?'*
>
> *'You mentioned the need for good communication skills and you have brought along a report to demonstrate your written skills. What do you believe to be the basis for good communication?'*
>
> *'You mentioned your understanding of the micro- and macro-economic issues. Could you expand on this? What do you believe are the micro- and macro-economic issues affecting our industry?'*
>
> *'I am interested in your report on comparative worth—it is a problem that we have wrestled with here from time to time. What did you come up with? How do you believe we should determine comparative worth?'*

Clearly these questions demonstrate that the interviewers have been listening and are interested in what you have to say. These questions should be taken as a positive sign. None of them should surprise you, and they should be covered in your preparation. Clearly to walk into the interview and to answer this question in the best possible way without any prior consideration and preparation is almost impossible. It is certainly too much to ask of yourself.

Whispering Death

This question can be used for even more than I have currently demonstrated. Many of us when appearing at an interview have what I would call a 'whispering death', that is, we have a weakness or more correctly a *perceived* weakness, in that it is an impression, not a fact. It never comes up during the interview but as soon as we leave the room the interviewers put their heads together and whisper about us in a way that excludes us from the job.

If your background is in the public sector and you are trying for work in the private sector, then 'no private sector experience' may well be your whispering death. For others among us 'over-qualified' may be the whispering death. 'Too old' is rarely directly a whispering death but what happens is that 'too old' gets translated into other whispering deaths such as 'won't stay up to date', 'will want to be the boss after day one', and 'won't get on with the younger staff'.

These are just some of the whispering deaths that come to mind; there are many others. If you have a whispering death area, and you do not attempt to redress it at the interview then you are merely going through the motions and are certainly not helping yourself to get the job. If you try to address the whispering death area in a confrontational way, then your 'likeability factor' will plummet, and that will not help either.

The easiest way of redressing whispering death issues is to design the 'Why you?' answer, and in particular the parts 'what the job needs' and 'this is me', to minimise any whispering death problem you may have.

Let's look at some of the examples of whispering deaths that I mentioned earlier and how they might be overcome. I coached a woman, Alice, who had been the Head of Nursing in a public hospital and who wanted to move to a private hospital. We were aware that the whispering death was likely to be 'no private hospital experience'. In designing the 'what the job needs' part of the 'Why you?' answer she prepared this:

> *'Another understanding that I believe is necessary to have in order to do this job well is that this is a* private *hospital; yes, it is a hospital, but it is also a business. Yes, they are patients, but at the same time they are customers and clients of the hospital, and while we need good patient care we also need good customer service.*
>
> *'Most clients in a private hospital are there on a discretionary basis; they are there by choice, either their own choice or the choice of their doctor. They could choose to go elsewhere, to other hospitals. What we need to achieve as a team—the medical, nursing and service staff—is that not only do they come back here the next time they need hospital service, but they also tell their friends to come here. In this way we can build a reputation that keeps us busy and, importantly, keeps the occupancy rate high, which keeps us all in work.'*

Later in the 'this is me' part of the answer Alice added:

> *'One of the things which attracts me to this position is the job satisfaction of being able to measure yourself in such a direct way. If we see a patient a second time it is because they were*

happy with the service the first time. If somebody mentions that they came on the recommendation of a friend it means that we are doing something right, and that is pleasing.'

Those of us who do not work in private hospitals may find it distasteful, even callous, to refer to patients in such a way. But I can tell you that this response was well received in the actual interview, as well as redressing the 'whispering death' issue in a pro-active, non-confrontational manner. It was much more difficult after the interview to whisper 'no private hospital experience' when Alice had articulated a clear private hospital philosophy. Remember that what the interviewers really want is not experience, but the lessons learned from that experience.

Another whispering death is being considered over-qualified for the position. This can happen when the applicant has no choice but to put all their qualifications on the résumé in the first place. Otherwise, the easiest way to overcome being considered over-qualified is to simply not list all your qualifications. A response to over-qualification as part of the 'what the job needs' part of the 'Why you?' question might be this:

> *'Another thing that this job needs is someone who is happy to contribute at the level that this job demands. It is no good having someone who does not have the skills and therefore finds the job too taxing, but neither is it any good having someone who believes that the job is really below their level and so acts like the boss from day one. This in its own way is just as debilitating to the productivity of the team as someone who does not have the skills to do the job.*
>
> *'I'm not suggesting that jobs cannot or should not be stepping stones to other work; but the important thing is to achieve for yourself and the team by doing the job you are in to the best of your ability.'*

Later, in the 'this is me' part of the answer, this person could in the space of a sentence or two demonstrate that they are such a person.

Another whispering death which sometimes comes up is, 'will not stay up to date'. If you think this may be a problem for you, you might say, in the 'what the job needs' part of your answer:

> *'One of the things that this job needs is the ability to stay up to date. This is such a dynamic field that standing still is falling behind.'*

Later in 'this is me':

> *'The main reason that this field has kept my interest over the years is that it is constantly changing, which of course has*

required me to constantly change with it. It has been a work life of continual learning, and what I know now is different to what I knew as recently as two years ago and in all probability will be different to what I will know in a further two years' time. To me this is the real excitement about working in this field.'

It would be very difficult to whisper about this person, 'would not stay up to date' when they left the room.

I hope by now that I have demonstrated how to use the 'Why you?' question to its fullest advantage. You cannot do this 'off the top of your head' at an interview, you must prepare for it.

Tell Me About Yourself

One word of warning: there is another question, or more correctly a direction, 'Tell me about yourself', which interviewees sometimes confuse with the 'Why you?' question. 'Tell me about yourself' is not another version of the 'Why you?' question; instead, it is a direct request for a display of 'likeability'. *I cannot like you if I do not know you. Tell me about yourself so that I can begin to know you and work out if I like you.* 'Tell me about yourself' is a very personal request, and so your response must, at least to start off with, reflect this. As you move through your answer it should become more and more focused on your working life.

Be careful not to waffle on while telling the interviewers about yourself. Some people give their life details to a minute degree. One man was cut off after ten minutes, when he was only up to grade two at primary school!

If I were asked this question my response would be along these lines:

'Well, I'm forty-one years old. I am English by birth, having been born in Leeds in the north of England. I come from a working class family. I am the oldest of three children and I have two brothers. At eleven I was fortunate to win a scholarship to the local grammar school; however, I did not finish my time at the school as we emigrated as a family to Australia.

'I was fourteen when we emigrated, and I still think it was one of the best things to happen to me. We moved to the outer eastern suburbs of Melbourne where I attended Croydon High School. I passed what was then HSC in 1973 and became the first person in my extended family to qualify for tertiary study.

'I became interested in the broader aspects of personnel work and staff management and so to this end I gained my

first full-time employment, as opposed to student casual and part-time work, as a trainee personnel clerk ...'

I would then give a short run-down on my working life, adding the more personal insights that are not on my résumé, such as what I liked about a particular job, the reasoning behind a career change and so on. I would finish along these lines:

'On a personal level: I am married, and I have one daughter, Tracy, who is eighteen and has just started university. If I have a passion in my life it is for fairness— have an abhorrence of racism and sexism in all their forms. I am a keen sports follower being an ex-soccer player and 400-metre runner. These days my sporting activity is restricted to following the Sydney Swans but I hope you don't hold that against me.'

Personal, but not too personal. No mention of any family or relationship problems, not that there are any, touch wood. It is as succinct as I can make it while at the same time attempting to give a clear insight into me, the likeable person. Other questions which are really asking 'tell me more about yourself', are the more obscure 'What makes you get up in the morning?' or 'Who are your heroes?'

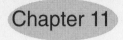

Chapter 11

LIST QUESTIONS

Most interviews contain at least one question to which the answer is a list. Usually these questions obviously request a list:

> *'What regulations do you know of that cover this area of work?'*

If you know of more than one regulation, then the answer will be a list. Other such questions are:

> *'What steps would you take in the following situation ...?'*

> *'What do you see as the benefits of ...?'*

> *'What do you feel will be the major changes in this industry within the next five years?'*

> *'What programs can you use?'*

> *'What do you see as your strengths?'*

Hopefully the answer to the last is a list. If you know of more than one step, benefit, program or change, then the answer will be in the form of a list.

Sometimes the list questions are not as obvious as this. One of the interviews that I sat in on was at a transport company looking for a courier driver. The details in this answer are particular to the city where I live, but the principles are the same in any city in the world. The employer interviewed many applicants. One of the questions asked of each applicant was:

'Let's say you get this job and you are in the city and you have a parcel to deliver to the suburb of Box Hill—how would you get there?'

I could virtually see the smile come across each interviewee's face as they realised that they knew the answer. It was as if they were thinking, 'Good! I know the way to Box Hill! I'm glad he didn't ask me how to get to McKinnon, as I'm not sure how to get there.' Nine out of ten interviewees leaned forward and confidently said 'Whitehorse Road', knowing it to be correct. Some said 'Canterbury Road' or 'Eastern Freeway', which are also technically correct, as there is more than one way from the city to Box Hill.

What the interviewees did not know was that the destination for each parcel was changed according to the address of the applicant. Each person was given an address near where they lived. The employer could fairly assume that the interviewee knew the answer before the question was asked. So why ask the question? Not to seek the information, that much is sure. To seek the wisdom, the insight and the understanding, of course. Although in this case the employer would have probably have articulated it as 'common-sense'.

As each interviewee said, 'Whitehorse Road', the interviewer would then say:

'There's been an accident on Whitehorse Road and consequently it is closed to traffic; which way would you go now?'

Most people replied in this way:

'Oh, if I knew that there was an accident because I heard it on the radio, or I bumped into the traffic jam, I would cut across to Canterbury Road.'

The employer then continued:

'All the traffic from Whitehorse Road is being detoured along Canterbury Road, consequently Canterbury Road is very slow.'

'Again if I knew that or came across it then I would cut right across to the Eastern Freeway; it is a bit longer but it would be a lot quicker.'

Whitehorse Road, Canterbury Road, Eastern Freeway—the answer was always going to be a list. You could volunteer a list or it would be extracted from you, but the answer would be a list.

The list question offers the clearest option at an interview of offering information or wisdom, and each time it will be the wisdom which is more impressive. The biggest and most common mistake that people make when answering the list question is that they make the first words out of their mouth the start of their list. This is natural if you see the list question merely as a request for information. Ask someone applying for an office position which computer software applications they know and you can just about count on them starting, 'Word for Windows, Excel ...' and so on.

The rules for answering any list question to the best advantage are clear. Make an introductory comment, as discussed earlier, then introduce your list, explain why there is a list and then explain why each of the items is on your list. It is hard to resist starting the answer with the beginning of your list, but do not do this under any circumstances.

If you happen to run into a person who only wants the information, then they will make this known either directly or through their body language and you can shorten your answer to suit; however, the rule of thumb should be start broad (not too broad) and work narrow.

Let's try the rules on our hidden list question for the courier:

> *'Let's say you got this job and you are in the city and you had a parcel to deliver to the suburb of Box Hill. How would you get there?'*

> *'Well, I've driven from the city to Box Hill on many occasions and there are a number of ways to get there. The most direct way is along Whitehorse Road but I find that between two-thirty and three-thirty there are so many school crossings on Whitehorse Road that it really slows down and during that time it is quicker to use Canterbury Road. If there are any hold-ups such as broken-down cars or road works on either Whitehorse or Canterbury then you are better off giving them both a wide berth and using the Eastern Freeway. It is further in distance but likely to be much quicker.*

> *'Wherever I'm going I always try and get there in the quickest possible time rather than the shortest distance. I*

would rather travel four kilometres further to get there ten minutes quicker.'

Compare this answer with 'Whitehorse Road'. This answer has wisdom, insight and understanding and therefore makes better use of the question. It starts with a comment, it introduces the list and it states why there is a list and why each of the routes are on the list. This particular answer also has the added bonus of finishing with a comment.

Let's face it, if you were asked to list relevant safety rules for a position and there were eight such rules and you managed to cite all eight, so what? Most telephone numbers are no more than eight digits long, but I'm not impressed when someone remembers a telephone number. I expect people to remember a telephone number, particularly when they knew they were going to be asked for it.

Do not fall into the trap of introducing the list by announcing the specific number of items on your list. If you say 'there are seven regulations' you will count them off and so will the interviewers. I have seen the fingers moving as they count down a list. If you get to six and can't think of the seventh, everybody knows that you forgot one. Worse still, if you think of a few more along the way and you get to nine then you will look silly. 'There are several' or 'there are a number' is a far safer way of introducing your list.

If you are applying for positions which necessitate you taking a portfolio of your work to the interview, treat the portfolio as a list and say why each item in the portfolio is there. Do not hand over a portfolio for the interviewers' perusal without 'selling' your work to them.

In your preparation for the interview, write out the answers to a few list questions which are relevant to the position.

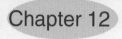

Chapter 12

THE HYPOTHETICAL QUESTION

Now we come to the dreaded 'what if?' question. You can always recognise this question: 'What would you do if you were successful in gaining this position and the following circumstance arose ...?'

Each occupation and industry seems to have its own cliché questions that get asked again and again. If you are in a customer service area the most commonly asked 'what if?' question is some derivative of 'What would you do if you had an angry customer?' If you are applying for a supervisor's position they tend to run along this line: 'What would you do if you were in this position and one of your staff started coming back from lunch late and they had obviously been drinking?'

Often the 'what if?' question is the most difficult and contrived question at interview. Contrived? Sometimes they are just so extreme as to be unrealistic. 'What would you do if you were the only person around and the sky was about to fall in?' Oh yes, being the only person around is another common element of the 'what if?' question.

Let's be quite clear about the 'what if?' question: even though the interviewer asks 'what would you do if ...?' *Do not under any circumstances tell them what you would do*. You cannot do well in this answer if you actually tell the interviewer what you would do. In fact it is more likely that you will appear blinkered in your thought, narrow-minded, and inflexible. Often if you tell them what you would do, the interviewers take a perverse delight in moving the goalposts, so that your answer looks silly or inappropriate.

I attended an interview being conducted by a large retail chain. They were interviewing for someone who moved from store to store conducting in-store promotions. One of the applicants was a woman who was doing very well until she got the 'what if' question.

In this particular case the 'what if?' question was a fairly obvious one, for which she should have had a good answer already prepared. She was asked:

> *'What would you do if you were successful in gaining this postion and you went to one store and the manager there said, "Thanks but no thanks. I don't agree with in-store promotions.I believe that they upset the rhythm of a store and that they give the customers unrealistic expectations. Good luck with the other stores, but not in my store."*
>
> *What would you do if this happened to you?'*

It seemed as if the interviewee thought to herself, *'They want to see how tough I can be. I'll be tough.'* She leaned forward, put a clenched fist on the small table between her and the interviewers, and said:

> *'I would demand that he participate in the program and if he still did not I would come back to head office and report him to the state manager.'*

She lost the job at that point. If she wanted to demonstrate toughness she certainly did that. In real life perhaps her approach would have been the only way of dealing with the issue, but surely such a strong stance should be a last and not a first resort. What about all the other options that she could have tried first: negotiating, problem solving, trialing, and even bribing, before demanding.

Another problem was her assumption that the manager was male when no gender had been mentioned. This may seem minor but it contributed to the perception that she was narrow-minded, particularly in an organisation that prided itself on the number of female managers it had.

It is very difficult to construct a 'what if?' question which is so clearly defined that there is only one correct response. Even the 'angry customer' scenario may have different responses.

Some customers are right to be angry because the standard of service has been poor. Other customers are unhappy because there has been a misunderstanding or a miscommunication. Still other customers are angry because they are 'professional' angry customers who believe that they will gain an unfair commercial advantage through appearing angry. You should deal with each of these customers in a different way, although some steps would be the same regardless of why the customer was angry, such as minimising the disruption by moving them away from other customers.

Some interviewees realise that there is more than one option available to them, but they are so intent on getting the 'right' answer that they start asking the interviewers questions in an attempt to narrow down the options to the 'right' one.

The classic 'what if?' question for child-care positions is:

> *'What would you do if you were here by yourself for a little while and one of the children came up to you and said that they felt sick?'*

The most common response to this question is:

> *'Well, I've still got the other children to consider and I can't neglect them, so if this happened to me I think I would ring the parents while still keeping my eyes on the other children.'*

You may find this response to be perfectly reasonable, but what usually happens is that the trap has been sprung and the interviewers now take a perverse delight in moving the goalposts and leaving the answer stranded.

> *'What if this child was the type of child who said they were sick each day just to gain attention?'*

> *'Oh, in that case I probably would do little more than give them a pat on the head and put them in a corner to keep my eyes on them to make sure that today was not the day when they were really sick.'*

Quite a good salvage under the circumstances, but the goalposts are about to be moved again as a different slant is put on the scenario:

> *'What if this child was showing symptoms of an illness that had been prevalent in the centre?'*

Some interviewees might respond to the original question with a series of questions of their own.

> *'Is this the sort of child who says that they are sick every day just to gain attention? No? Does this child have any allergies that I should know about? No? Is this child on any medication? No? Is there a contagious illness that*

has been evident in the centre that I might recognise the symptoms of? No? Is this child blue in the face?'

These questions are asked to try to narrow down the possibilities so that the 'right' answer may be given. But it is not a good idea to start asking the interviewers questions about their question, unless you need simple clarification; most interviewers will find this irritating. A better approach is to include all the possibilities into your own answer.

When someone asks 'What would you do if ...?', the reality is they do not want to know what you would do. What they want to know is, how do you think? How do you reason? On what basis do you make decisions? If there was ever a question which demanded that you think out loud (or at least appear to think out loud, the real thinking having been in your interview preparation), this is it.

The best response to the 'what if?' question is to treat it as a list question, a list of your options. The structure to the answer then should look like this: a comment, the introduction to the list, why there is a list, why each of the items is on the list, a finishing comment. The child-care worker could have introduced the answer in this way:

> *'It would be an unusual day when at least one of the children didn't say that they were feeling sick, even if they weren't. There are a number of things that I might do, depending on the exact situation. If the child was the type of child who was known to claim sickness to gain attention ..., However, if this child ...'*

The answer would then run through all the possible options. A finishing comment might be:

> *'I believe the secret in these situations is to deal with them safely with a minimum of fuss, but if I were to err, I would rather err on the side of safety. I would rather ring an ambulance and find out it was not necessary that not ring one and find out that it was.'*

This structure allows you to display your wisdom, insight and understanding rather than just describe what you would do. Here is another 'what if' situation:

> *'What would you do if you were successful in gaining this*

> *supervisor's position and after you had been here for a*
> *short time, one of your staff started coming back from*
> *lunch late and had obviously been drinking?'*

I have seen this type of question asked on numerous occasions.
The most common response is:

> *'I would counsel him or her.'*

Great answer, four words! There is no wisdom in this answer and it
may well provoke the following response as the goalposts are
moved:

> *'Really? What if this person had been a good staff*
> *member for many years and recently they had separated*
> *from their partner of many years, would you still counsel*
> *them?'*

If you were to put your answer to the original question through the
suggested structure for answers to this type of question it might
sound like this (after the compulsory pause, assumption of the
thinking pose and repeating the question out loud, as discussed
earlier):

> *'Can I say at the outset that if I had been in the job for*
> *any length of time I would be very disappointed that my*
> *relationship with any staff member was such that this sort*
> *of behaviour took place. It would make me consider the*
> *quality of my work as supervisor and leader in the area.*
> *'Having said that, there are a number of things that I*
> *might do depending on the exact circumstances.*
> *'If this was a person who had been a good reliable staff*
> *member for a long time and their behaviour was out of*
> *character I would be interested as to why this behaviour*
> *was suddenly taking place. I would speak to the person*
> *quietly, or perhaps to a friend of theirs if I knew they were*
> *close to someone at work. If it turned out the behaviour*
> *was a symptom of some personal trauma I would see if*
> *we could help in some way as a first step, before making it*
> *a disciplinary matter. Perhaps I could enlist some help*
> *from an alcohol and drug counsellor.*
> *'If this was not the case, then as a first step I might*
> *make some passing comment indicating that the behaviour*

was not going unnoticed. I find that sometimes this is all staff need to adjust their own behaviour. If this did not work, I believe it would be my responsibility to ensure that all staff knew that our standards of punctuality will be maintained. I would make these standards quite clear to the staff member.

'If this too did not work or I found that this had already been made clear in the past, then I would start a formal disciplinary process, keeping notes at each stage, which might lead to dismissal. Sometimes dismissal is unavoidable, but I always see it as a defeat, personally, that I was not able to turn a person around at the early stages.

'One thing I have learned from these situations is to deal with them as soon as they come to your attention. Very rarely will they just go away; they will fester and start affecting other staff. If there is a hard decision to make, do it as soon as you realise it has to be made—sitting on it will not make it any easier.'

In recent years the 'why you?' question has changed. Instead of being hypothetical, it has become experiential. Instead of being asked 'what if ...?', interviewees are being directed, 'Tell me about a problem you had and how you overcame it.' It is still the 'what if?' question, but the interviewers are too lazy to think of a situation for themselves, and leave it up to you. This possibility should be covered in your preparation.

If you are asked an experiential type of question, don't forget to include the options available to you in dealing with your problem. Many interviewees make this mistake; they describe the problem and then immediately move on to how they fixed it. In doing this they are being unfair to themselves, underselling themselves, because this could not be what happened in real life. In real life you recognise a problem, you sit down and consider your options, and finally choose the one that seems best.

The ideal structure of this answer would be: comment, problem, and then: 'When thinking about the problem I knew I had a number of options. I could do this ..., this ..., or this ...; however, what I chose to do was this ... for these reasons ...'

The value to you of being asked a hypothetical question at an interview is not that it provides you with an opportunity to say what you would do, but that it allows you to demonstrate the wisdom, the insight and the understanding that you would bring to the situation.

Chapter 13

STRENGTHS AND WEAKNESSES

Strengths

The 'strengths' question that I have touched on earlier is a fair question. The question usually comes to you directly as, 'What do you see as your strengths in regard to this position?' I have no problem with this question, as essentially it is challenging you to sell yourself for the job. It is an invitation to put forward your good points in relation to the job being applied for and as such should be a question you look forward to. Unfortunately, many interviewees do not take full advantage of this question. The most common mistake is to run through a list of adjectives:

> 'I'm conscientious, hardworking, loyal, honest, reliable, results-oriented ...'

and perhaps three or four other adjectives you found in the dictionary which you thought would sound good at the interview. This is as meaningless and platitudinous when said, as it is when written on résumés.

What sells at an interview? By now you should know this so clearly that you can recite it in your sleep: wisdom, insight and understanding. There is no wisdom, insight, or understanding in reciting a list of adjectives and that is why the example above is a poor answer.

It should be a list question, and for your sake I hope it is. If you believe you have few or no strengths, you will have a hard time at the interview. When considering what your strengths are, be your own best friend: be generous to yourself.

As we discussed, the way to approach list questions is to comment, introduce your list, say why there is a list and then why each of your items is on your list.

A good comment as an introduction to listing your strengths might sound like this:

> '*I am always uncomfortable talking about what I believe are my good points. I believe that actions speak louder than words and I would prefer to demonstrate my strengths than talk about them. Having said that, I do think that I have a number of strengths which this position needs.*'

This would come after the pause, the thinking pose and the audible pondering, 'What do I see as my strengths?' I have found this start the best way to prevent yourself from appearing conceited. Many interviewees are not comfortable talking about their strengths because they are afraid that they will appear conceited, and if you feel this way the above approach will prove useful.

After this beginning you should then go on to introduce each of your strengths and, importantly, after each strength to explain why that strength is relevant to the position that you are being interviewed for. Other than honesty, which I mentioned earlier, I do not want to suggest what your strengths should be, as you know them best. Some of the list of adjectives which I mentioned earlier such as hard-working, conscientious and loyal may well be good strengths to have, providing they are sold correctly, and the way to do that is to demonstrate why each particular strength is relevant to the job.

> '*One of my strengths is that I am hard-working, and in this particular position that is important because it is so busy, particularly towards the end of the month, that if you got behind it would be very difficult to catch up and the standard of service we offer would start to decline. It is important in this job to be able to get the quantity out as well as the quality.*'

This generic response for 'hard-working' could be applicable to a wide range of jobs and as part of a broader list of strengths it is good, because not only does it indicate a strength of the speaker quite clearly, but it promotes that strength as being particularly necessary, showing insight into the position. There is no point in including strengths on your list that you cannot demonstrate are relevant to the job.

One unusual strength that I have found 'sells' very well for positions with finance or security components is to be pedantic!

> '*One of what I believe to be my strengths is a quality that not many people like owning up to, and that is that I am pedantic when necessary. Many people would shy away from describing themselves in this way but I believe that in any organisation someone has to take the responsibility to watch all the details. It*

balances out all of the free-flowing, fast thinking staff and sometimes keeps them grounded. There has to be someone willing to say that near enough is not good enough and that there are areas where the 'i's have to be dotted and the 't's crossed. It seems to me that the person with this attribute is best placed in Accounts (Security).

Remember that one of your strengths should always be your honesty.

Weaknesses

The strengths question is a good, fair question and I have no problem with it. However, the weaknesses question is a nasty question. It is an unfair question and should never be asked. This question asks honest people to hang themselves, and sometimes they do. The best place to include honesty in your interview is in the strengths question. The worst place for it is in the weaknesses question.

I am not one for telling lies at an interview, except in reply to unfair questions. That is, those questions where you may pay a penalty for being honest. It is wrong for any question at an interview to demand that the interviewee should pay a penalty for being honest. Essentially the 'weaknesses' question is an invitation to give the interviewer a reason why you should not get the job.

At one interview a man was asked what he saw as his major weakness. After an uncomfortable pause he said, 'To be perfectly honest, I'm not famous for getting things finished.' This is an honest answer, indeed. This is a breathtakingly honest answer. This man is either one of the most honest people I have ever met, or the most stupid. He had 'honested' himself right out the door. The interviewers could not recommend someone who had openly told them that they started things but did not finish them.

The irony was that the man's name was Frank. Frank had been too frank. A lot of fun was had at Frank's expense throughout the remainder of the interviews. Whenever there was a flat spot (and no other interviewees were around) one of the interviewers would say, 'To be perfectly honest, I'm an axe murderer', and everyone would laugh out loud. The sad thing is that we interviewed four other applicants for the position and they possibly had the same problem, but they were just not silly enough to tell us so. The Frank story is an extreme example but it serves to illustrate the point well.

I recently coached a woman who had the weakness, or the 'whispering death', of having no direct experience in the work she wanted to do. She had worked in related areas but not directly in the one she was applying for. I changed her résumé so that it told of the lessons she had learned rather than her experience. I was confident that unless the reader of the résumé knew what to look for or was particularly thorough they would not realise that my client had no direct experience. During the preparation for the interview I asked her what she would say when they asked what her weakness was, and she replied:

'That's easy, I'll just tell them that I have no direct experience.'

I shook my head in despair. She was going to undo all the good work I had done on her résumé. Her reply was the equivalent of someone selling a used car, who said to potential buyers, 'Did I tell you that the gear-box is making strange noises? They are very expensive to fix.'

In the end it is 'buyer beware.' It is the buyer's (interviewer's) job to find the faults, not the seller's (interviewee's) job to reveal them. If after stating her weakness, the woman in question was still being considered for the job along with one other applicant, one of the interviewers could say, 'By her own admission she has no direct experience', and use her own words to rule her out. Never give the interviewers such ammunition.

You must indicate that you have some fault. You may try to get away with saying that you have no fault you are aware of, but that may provoke the following:

'What do you see as your weakness?'
'I am not aware of any weaknesses that I have.'
'So you are perfect, are you?'
'No, I didn't say that I am perfect.'
'So you have weaknesses but you are just not sure what they are. Do you think that this in itself is a weakness?'

You are in a hole at this stage. Even if you are going to attempt to get by with no weakness, it is nice to have one handy if it is called for.

In constructing an answer to the weakness question there are some rules to follow. Clearly it is a question that demands a pause and an audible consideration of the question. You do not want to seem to be so close to your weaknesses that you know them off by heart, and reply as soon as the question is asked, 'Oh weaknesses—let me tell you.'

The pause while you are considering your weakness is an easy place to introduce humour. In fact this is the best time during an interview to use humour. You might say, 'What is my weakness—besides chocolate?' or 'besides milkshakes'. It is not very funny, but it is safe and it will receive a polite smile or snigger and a little tick in the box marked 'Sense of Humour'. After this you must continue with a 'real' weakness.

This is as far as you can take humour at this time. Some have tried to take it further with disastrous results, for instance:

'Weakness! Gee, this is going to be a long interview, isn't it.'

This is lead balloon territory.

You must indicate at least one weakness. Unlike the strengths question the answer is not a list; you can usually get away with one. If you have a weakness that you know about, why is it that you have not fixed it? To overcome this dilemma, the best thing to say after your pause is:

'I prefer to see it as something that I am still working on.'

From here the path through the answer should be, 'In the past, I have had this problem' (pausing here to draw a two-sentence picture of how the problem manifested itself) '... and this is what I have learned from the problem ... and this is how I now try to respond.' There are any number of weaknesses that can be safely put through this format.

What is the best use to the interviewee of the question, 'What do you see as your weakness?' It is to take the opportunity to point out that you can learn your lessons. Use the question to demonstrate that you are flexible and adaptable when necessary.

One response to this question is:

'My weakness is that I work too many hours of unpaid overtime.'

A good try, but it won't work. I am not saying that you cannot have this problem. I am saying that you have to sell it better. Let's put this problem through the suggested structure.

'I prefer to think of it as something that I am still working on. I think it's true that in the past I have become overly focused on some work matters to the exclusion of everything else. This has caused me some problems, and there have been times when my family has said to me: "You've been home from work for three hours now—put it down, let it go." From this I have learned that while there is a time for focusing to the exclusion of everything else there also has to be a time for family and for recreation. If not, in the end you burn out and you are no good to anyone. I think I'm much better at getting the balance right these days.'

The problem here is still of working too many unpaid hours of overtime: it's just sold much better.

The bottom line on the 'weakness' response is to use the structure suggested to construct a response that you can give with a straight face. If that response bears no resemblance to real life, then that is the price the interviewers pay for asking an unfair question. Above all, do not let the interviewers invite you to give a reason why you should not get the job.

Chapter 14

'WHERE ARE YOU GOING?'

One of the most difficult questions to answer at an interview is, 'Where do you see yourself in five (two, three, four, ten) years' time?' This question is usually only asked in interviews for white collar, professional and semi-professional jobs.

It can be easy to answer this question if you know that the interviewers are looking for an ambitious go-getter, as all you have to do is suggest a level that such a person would be achieving in five years. On the other hand, if you know that the interviewers are looking for someone who is prepared to stay at the same level for some time, it is equally easy to construct the 'right' answer.

There was a time when you could side-step this question by smiling and saying, '*Your* position looks good to me,' but this was never a very good response and the unemployment situation now causes many interviewers to be threatened by it.

The difficulty with this question is that in most of cases you don't know what reply the interviewers want to hear. If you are ringing the organisation before your interview to do some 'home-work' this may be a question to add to your list: 'Where do you see the person who gets this job in five years' time?'

Without this information you have a fifty-fifty chance of getting the answer right. I'm not sure that those odds are good enough to take a guess. One way of avoiding this dilemma that I have found successful is to not attach a position or a level to where you may be in five years' time, but instead to give a more personal response:

> '*I am a person who requires job satisfaction to be happy and productive in my work and this is what I have set my mind on achieving in the medium term. For me to have job satisfaction I need a few things. I need to be working to my potential, if not*

*being stretched, and I need to be busy. I need to be contributing
and to be recognised for that contribution. I need to be valued
by the organisation and my peers. I need involvement to the
extent that work becomes part of life and not just an attach-
ment to it.*

*'You might think that I am asking a lot but this is the goal I
have set myself and I hope to achieve within five years. To a
great extent the actual position is secondary. Some people are
not happy unless they achieve a certain power or a certain
salary, but to me job satisfaction is the most important thing. If
you have a satisfying job you are lucky regardless of where you
are on the ladder—the top, the middle or the bottom. I believe if
you enjoy your job and you do it well everything else flows from
that.'*

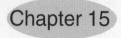Chapter 15

ENDING THE
INTERVIEW

Earlier we looked at primacy and recency in relation to interviews and noted how important the first impression, primacy, is. The end of the interview, recency, is also important.

The end of the interview is usually signalled by the interviewers asking, 'Is there anything else that you would like to add?' If this opportunity is not offered to you, you can create it yourself: 'Before we finish there is something else that I would like to say.' It is an important thing to do—this is the place to ask for the job. **Do not leave the room without asking for the job.**

What you would really like to say is what you are probably thinking:

> *Yes, this is my life. Do not dismiss me lightly. Give me every due consideration. Do not wave me away with the back of your hand.*

Of course if we said this, the likeability factor would plummet, and this would not help our cause. The way to make these points is to borrow from the answer for the 'why you?' question:

> *'Yes, this position is important to me. I have not applied for it lightly. I have not applied for it just because it is a job and I need a job. I have not applied just to see how I will go. I have applied only after careful consideration of how important the job is, and what qualities it needs to be successful and matching myself to those needs. I have applied for this position only because I believe that I can make a valuable contribution.'*

After the 'anything else to add?' offer, the interviewer's part of the interview is over and now it is likely that control will be offered to the interviewee. 'Do you have any questions?'

Many interviewees make a major mistake here and undo a lot of their good work. **Be quite clear about this; do not ask any questions about the job.** It is a nonsense and illogical to do so. The interview is over, finished, gone. No information about the position can help you now. Some interviewees even go as far as asking, 'Could you tell me more about the job?' The mistaken belief is that this question will demonstrate interest and enthusiasm. It will not; it will suggest that you do not even know what you have applied for. It will show that you have not done your homework.

Of course some discretion can be used. If there is something you need to know that you just could not find out before the interview, and the answer is crucial to your decision as to whether to accept the job if you are offered it, then by all means ask the question. But don't ask a question just because you feel you should.

The way to get full value from 'any questions?' is to say:

> *'I don't have any questions because I checked the job out thoroughly before applying.'*

You might ask a rhetorical question:

> *'I understand the previous occupant for the position received an early promotion?'*
> *'I understand that you are planning to expand into other areas in the near future?'*
> *'I understand that you use an IBM local area network?'*

Of course none of these are real questions, but instead demonstrate the results of some homework.

You can also ask any question about the interview process:

> *'When will you be making a decision?'*
> *'When will you want the successful candidate to start?'*

Some jobs have a fixed pay rate known beforehand, that is, it is set and not negotiable. Others have much broader salary parameters and the final figure will be determined by negotiation. If you are in the second group, try not to negotiate salary conditions until you are offered the job. It is not always possible to avoid this negotiation, but if you negotiate without having been offered the job the pressure to go low is enormous. If the interviewer asks:

> *'What salary do you envisage if you were successful?'*

You could reply:

> *'I'm happy to start on the industry standard, perhaps with a review built in for when I have demonstrated that I am worth more than that.'*

You are unlikely to avoid discussing the issue as easily as this. Such an answer is likely to solicit the following response:

'And what do you believe is the industry standard?'

The idea now is to put forward a range of salary levels encompassing the figure that you believe is the fair one. If you believe a fair salary for the position is $42 000 but you are prepared to accept $39 000, the range to put forward would be $39 000–$45 000. If later you are offered the position, you are much better placed to negotiate the deal that you want. It is your task to get the starting salary as close as you can to $45 000, and theirs to get you as close as possible to $39 000.

After your questions and the salary discussion, the interview is over. You should thank the interviewers for their time, put your jacket back on if you are a man or pull the shirt sleeves down if you are a woman, put the documents back in your briefcase and make your exit. I have seen some interviewees say at this stage, 'Are there any concerns about my suitability for the position that I can clarify for you?' but I have never seen this approach to be successful and I counsel against it. The best leaving statement is the simple, 'Look forward to hearing from you soon.' And then you should leave. Remember to keep your composure until you are well out of sight of the building.

A recent trend has been for the interviewee to send a follow-up letter the next day thanking the employers for the interview. While I can see no harm in this, I haven't seen any tangible benefits from this strategy and so don't recommend it.

Chapter 16

A FINAL REMINDER

In closing I would like to repeat what I said in the beginning. Interviews are not about the best person for the job—they can't be. Interviews are about who interviews best, about who appears to be the best. The abilities, capacity and worth that you take into the interview room will never be tested; only your ability to interview will be.

If you are not interviewing well at the moment, if you are not happy with your success rate, then some things need to change. In this book I hope I have shown where those changes can take place. But winning jobs is not a finite science, and I am not the source of all knowledge in this area. In the end I don't have to be happy with your interview performance; you do.

I have two hopes:

✔ That the next time you hear a question at an interview you don't think, 'What's the right answer?' but, 'How do I best use this question to my advantage?'

✔ That when you are successful and are in an important job you will not forget that there are many good workers who are denied an opportunity because they are poor interviewees. You will have a chance to help change the system to make it fairer for all.

Good luck in your future interviews.